Awakening Beauty

An illustrated look at mankind's love and hatred of beauty

by

Anthony Napoleon, Ph.D.

"Awakening Beauty," by Anthony Napoleon. ISBN 1-58939-378-3

Published 2003 by Virtualbookworm.com Publishing Inc., P.O. Box 9949, College Station, TX , 77842, US. © 2003 Anthony Napoleon. All rights reserved. No part of this publication may be reproduced, stored in a retrieval system, or transmitted in any form or by any means, electronic, mechanical, recording or otherwise, without the prior written permission of Anthony Napoleon.

Manufactured in the United States of America.

Table of Contents

Introduction

Beauty is one of those subjects that always gets attention. My own fascination with the subject came from my attraction to beautiful women. Much to my surprise, however, it didn't take long before I became as interested in what was behind the beautiful visage as I was with the package it came in. Beauty affects virtually every aspect of our emotional and cultural life. Even our physical health is impacted by beauty. On the other hand, when it comes to appreciating the profound importance of beauty, virtually no other subject is as well protected by a mantle of denial and dismissiveness. It seems to be accepted that serious authors and researchers don't write about beauty. The subject area, like beauty itself, is presumed to be only skin deep.

Beauty, as a subject area, is a seamless tapestry made up of many different colors, but always a part of the same fabric. This seamless quality to the subject area is reflected in this book. When we discuss plastic surgery, for example, we end up exploring beauty's relationship to sexuality. And when we explore the relationship between sexuality and beauty, we end up discussing the rich man/pretty woman connection.

My expertise on the subject of beauty is the culmination of twenty years of formal study and professional work. In the late 1980's I held a medical psychology fellowship in plastic surgery. My work in plastic surgery afforded me the opportunity to study, in depth, both patients and surgical procedures. Before that, I wrote a dissertation on the relationship between physical attractiveness, personality and family environment. In 1980 I conducted research at a large mental hospital in the Midwest, in an effort to ferret out the connection between physical attractiveness and mental illness. For seven years I held a position at a consulting firm as a developer, writer and teacher of various subjects related to beauty and attractiveness, with the sole purpose of increasing both for our clients. I have judged over 100 beauty pageants, including The Miss and Mrs. California USA Beauty Pageants. Ten years after the original publication of my research which identified, for the first time, the personalities of patients who undergo plastic surgery, I still receive requests from all over the world for reprints from surgeons and students interested in the relationship between beauty and personality.

My work in forensics, especially in the courtroom, has impressed upon me the value that comes from understanding beauty. After twenty years of study and work in the area, I say with some conviction that anyone who thinks that beauty is only skin deep hasn't thought a lot about the subject. Understanding beauty provides a window into the soul of man. No matter who you are, your life has been changed by beauty.

Chapter I: Beautiful Women

There are two kinds of women: beautiful women, and women who want or have wanted to be beautiful. Beautiful women and those who want to be beautiful have spawned a multi-billion dollar beauty industry, an industry which sells hair color, plastic surgery, and everything imaginable in between. Beautiful women both feel and can arouse deep emotion, but it is not always positive emotion. For example, beautiful women are forever chasing greater beauty, while at the same time anxiously trying to fend off the effects of aging. Consider that unattractive women in pursuit of beauty often hate, with a passion, those women who already possess the beauty they so desperately desire.

Men, like women, are profoundly affected by beauty. Consider the shared human experience which gave rise to the song: *When You're in Love with a Beautiful Woman*, made popular by the band Dr. Hook:

When you're in love with a beautiful woman, it's hard. When you're in love with a beautiful woman, you know it's hard, cause everybody wants her, everybody loves her, everybody wants to take your baby home.

When you're in love with a beautiful woman, you watch your friends. When you're in love with a beautiful woman, it never ends, you know that is crazy and you wanna trust her, then somebody hangs up when you answer the phone. When you're in love with a beautiful woman, you go it alone.

Maybe it's just an ego problem, problem is that I've been fooled before by fair-weather friends and faint hearted lovers, and every time it happens it just convinces me more.

When you're in love with a beautiful woman, you watch her eyes. When you're in love with a beautiful woman, you look for lies,' cause everybody tempts her everybody tells her she's the most beautiful woman they know. When you're in love with a beautiful woman, you go it alone.

Or how about the song *If You Want to be Happy*, by Jimmy Soul, which topped the charts in 1963. This song gives voice to what many men come to feel after years and years of frustration dealing with beautiful women.

If you wanna be happy for the rest of your life,

never make a pretty woman your wife, so from my personal point of view, get an ugly girl to marry you.

A pretty woman makes her husband look small.
And very often causes his downfall. As soon as he marries her, then she starts to do the things that will break his heart.

But if you make an ugly woman your wife,
you'll be happy for the rest of your life. An ugly woman cooks her meals on time; she'll always give you peace of mind.

Don't let your friends say you have no taste.
Go ahead and marry anyway, though her face is ugly, her eyes don't match, take it from me she's a better catch.

Say man, hey baby, saw your wife the other day.
Yeah? Yeah, she's ugly. Yeah, she's ugly but she sure can cook. Yeah? Alright.

Men are inherently attracted to beautiful women, but as these song lyrics poignantly illustrate, men also mistrust beautiful women and often harbor many negative feelings about them. This love-hate relationship is difficult for men to navigate, but imagine how confusing and painful it is for women. After all, women strive to be physically attractive; yet, when they achieve it, more often than not, they bemoan the fact that men are just interested in them for their looks or mistrust them because they are beautiful. Marilyn Monroe summed up her feelings about beauty on the night she committed suicide. According to author Anthony Summers, Marilyn called her psychiatrist on the night of her death and complained that here she was, the most beautiful woman in the world, and she didn't even have a date for Saturday night.

Defining Beauty

What constitutes beauty? The short answer is that beauty is defined by genetic and culturally based ideals, tempered with some minor variations in personal taste. Both nature and nurture define our ideals of beauty. The biologically based determinants of beauty include such variables as symmetry, consistency of texture and color, lucidity in form, and proportionality.

Environmental influences shape our genetic predispositions to find certain characteristics beautiful. For example, the sixty years since World War II heralded a transition from the more full-figured Hollywood movie stars of the 1940s and 50s, to the often gaunt and anorexic stars of the early twenty-first century, all the while waist to hip ratios remained the same. But don't think that because culture helps to define what we think is beautiful, that our definition of beauty is significantly influenced by individualized tastes that vary significantly from one person to another.

My own research, along with others, has refuted the accepted idea that "beauty is in the eye of the beholder," a notion that suggests that each and every person has their own very different and individualized definition of what is beautiful. Notwithstanding the empirical research on the subject, a short jaunt along the path of logical reasoning illustrates that what constitutes beauty may not be subject to great differences in individualized taste. The fact that there are beautiful women, recognized all over the world for their beauty, demonstrates that significant numbers of people agree on what is and what is not beautiful.

Conversely, the fact that people agree that there are unattractive women, recognized everywhere as unattractive, is another way of illustrating the same principle. If we all had a unique, individualized standard of beauty; that is, "beauty is in the eye of the beholder," not enough of us could agree and there would be no "beautiful" women.

Learning What is Beautiful

One hundred years ago, the *model du jour* belonged to the fashion industry and its patrons in Paris and New York. Today, thanks to technology that makes possible world-wide media distribution, the *model du jour* belongs to the world. The images we see and the sounds we hear, without exception, are dominated—virtually permeated in every way—by an obsessive emphasis and focus upon beauty. The effect is profound; especially considering that exposure to the media, in its various forms, begins very early and reaches almost everyone.

The following data from a Federal Trade Commission Survey, spanning May to July, 2000, and a 1999 Kaiser Family Foundation report entitled *Kids and Media*, illustrates children's ever-increasing access to various media. In 1970, 35% of homes in the United States had more than one TV set. Six percent of sixth graders had a TV in their bedrooms. Compare those figures with the 1999 data, where 88% of homes had more than one TV set and 77% of sixth-graders had a TV in their rooms. The average child in the United States grows up in a home with three TVs, three tape players, three radios, two VCRs, two CD players, one video game system and one computer. The television is usually on during meals in 58% of homes with children.

Two-thirds of children eight years and older have TVs in their bedrooms. One out of five also has a computer in their bedroom. Children ages 8-13 years of age spend six and three-quarter hours daily plugged into various media, more than those in any other age group. In a typical week, children spend an average of more than 19 hours watching TV, more than 10 hours listening to music, more than 5 hours reading for pleasure, about 2 and one-half hours using computers for fun, and more than 2 hours playing video games.

Various media depictions of what is and what is not attractive become the ideal standard of beauty for girls and boys coming of age. "Be a model or look like one" is the slogan for a modeling school. It may as well be the mantra for virtually every young woman coming of age in the civilized world where obtaining basic necessities does not occupy all of her attention.

Gaining Access to the Media

Beauty can trump virtually any other quality or characteristic when it comes to gaining access to the media. "The 100 Best Looks," (PHOTO CREDIT FROM "US" WEEKLY) "The World's Most Beautiful Women," "The Best Dressed Women in America," and a host of other beauty-related lists, understandably provide access to the media for its members. But beauty has a way of providing access to the media even when your chosen profession has nothing, per se, to do with how you look. Take, for example, tennis player Anna Kournikova. Anna Kournikova is a professional tennis player who made the cover of Sport's Illustrated and Tennis Weekly without having ever won a professional tournament. (SEE PHOTOS OF ANNA KOURNIKOVA) Observers of professional tennis are quick to compare the media attention afforded Ms. Kournikova to the relatively sparse media coverage given such players as Lindsay Davenport, whose accomplishments in tennis include, among others: The 2000 Australian Open Championship; 1999 Wimbledon Championship; 1998 U.S. Open Championship; and The 1996 Olympic Championship. (SEE PHOTOS OF LINDSAY DAVENPORT)

When the "model" and the sports themes are joined, as was the case when professional tennis player Martina Hingis posed for her photo shoot, notwithstanding the tennis racquet held by Ms. Hingis, it is clear to the consumer which takes precedence: beauty or athletic achievement. (SEE PHOTOS OF MARTINA HINGIS)

Disparate media coverage is nothing new to women's sport. Gabriela Sabatini and Martina Navritilova were big draws, but for different reasons, in an earlier generation of tennis players. Gabriela got a disproportionate amount of media attention because, once again, she was more attractive than the athletically superior Martina Navritilova. In the 1970's, Laura Baugh was the "model" player on the women's professional golf tour. Baugh, a beautiful blond, was reputed to get much more up-front guarantee money than her peers, who were much better at the game of golf.

Jenny Thompson, an Olympic swimmer who has excelled in her sport, posed semi-nude in "Sport's Illustrated" magazine. A casual observer looking at that photo would not conclude that the "model" in the photo was primarily chosen for her athletic prowess. (SEE PHOTO OF JENNY THOMPSON)

Brandi Chastain, a renowned soccer player, had assets other than her soccer abilities emphasized when she appeared in "Gear" magazine. (SEE PHOTOS OF BRANDI CHASTAIN) The bottom line is that beauty sells, and it generally sells more than pure athletic performance, at least

One of Many Magazine Covers Related to Beauty

Anna Kournikova

Various Photos of Anna Kournikova

Lindsay Davenport

Lindsay Davenport

Lindsay Davenport with Wimbleton Cup

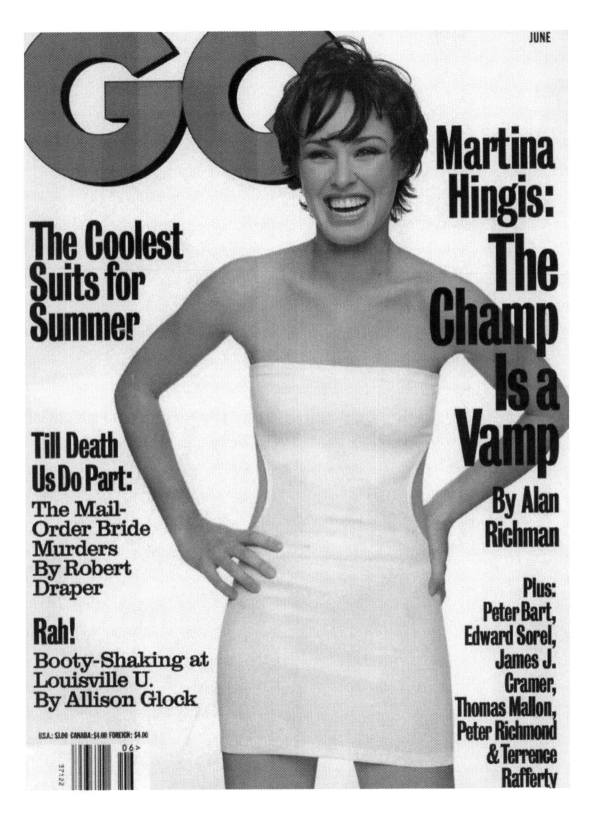

Martina Hingis

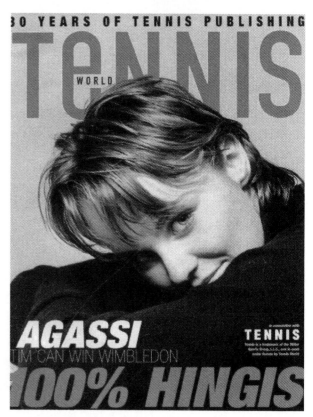

Martina Hingis

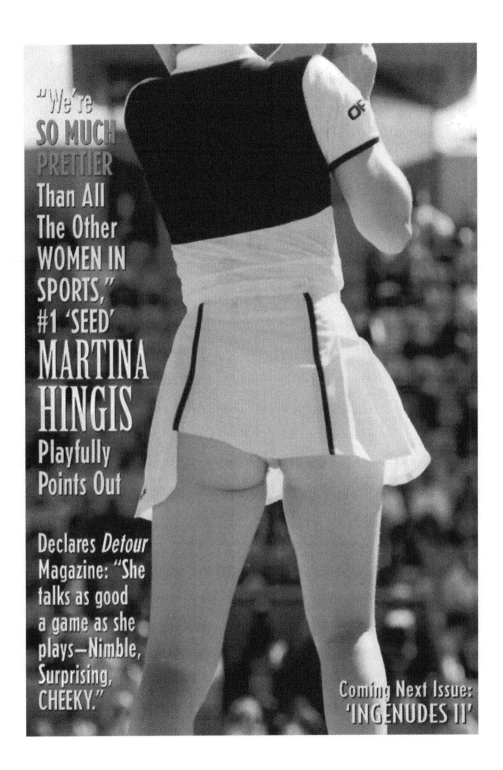

"We're **SO MUCH** PRETTIER Than All The Other WOMEN IN SPORTS," #1 'SEED' **MARTINA HINGIS** Playfully Points Out

Declares *Detour* Magazine: "She talks as good a game as she plays—Nimble, Surprising, CHEEKY."

Coming Next Issue: 'INGENUDES II'

Satirical Magazine Cover Referencing
Martina Hingis

Jenny Thompson in *Sports Illustrated*

Brandi Chastain in *Gear* Magazine

Brandi Chastain from *Gear* Magazine

when it comes to female athletes. It was more than coincidence that when Reebok signed tennis player Venus Williams to a $40-million plus contract, the marketing men and women at the shoe maker dressed Venus in a spaghetti-strap top that seemed intent on falling down on the tennis court. Not to be outdone by her sister, Serena Williams wore a skin-tight Lycra suit emblazoned with her sponsor's (Puma) logo at the 2002 U.S. Open. (SEE PHOTO CREDITS OF SERENA AND VENUS WILLIAMS) "It makes me run faster and jump higher and it's really sexy. It really sticks to what type of shape you have. If you don't have a decent shape, this isn't the best outfit to have," said Serena.

The Digital Generation

The digital revolution is leaving its unique fingerprint upon the subject of beauty. Teenage boys are falling in love with digitally created depictions of large-breasted, long-legged, unnaturally thin-waisted heroines depicted in video games. Take, for example, Lara Croft, the gun-toting beauty who stars in the video game "Tomb Raider." Miss Croft has captured the love interest of many a young member of the digital generation. (SEE DRAWING OF LARA CROFT)

Lara has disproportionately large and firm breasts; she has a peculiarly thin and narrow waist, disproportionately long legs, very large and full lips and a curvaceous derriere. She also is not real, in the sense that she is not made of flesh and blood and her proportions are certainly not human. Lara's thighs are bigger than her waist, and her waist is narrower than her face. If Lara went shopping she would certainly have to have her clothes tailored, unless she could find pants off the rack with a 36 inseam and a 12-inch waist.

The character was originally created by Toby Gard. Mr. Gard, though he is the creator of Lara Croft and the video game "Tomb Raider" that gave Lara her start, retains no rights to the character or the game. Adrian Smith is the current "creator" of Ms Croft. Smith was interviewed by Scott Steinberg, a freelance writer who covers the video gaming world, in the fall of 2000. He asked Lara's creator why he thought she was so popular. Reportedly, according to Mr. Steinberg, Mr. Smith told him, "Lara's a real woman, someone you could sit next to on the bus." I don't know what bus route Mr. Smith takes, but unless it is one of those bus routes that traverse the desert between Las Vegas and Area 51, I would be skeptical about finding anyone riding the bus who remotely resembles Lara Croft. According to Steinberg, a fan of Lara's cycled from Denmark to England because he wanted to meet her. All of this would be less than serious if it were not for the fact that Lara has become not only an ideal for how a young woman's body can look, but how it *should* look. Teenage boys all over the world compare the girl next door to Lara Croft. Further-more, it should be remembered that the video gaming industry posted profits greater than American movie box office receipts in 1998 and again in the year 2001.

If one moves to the R-rated world of animation one finds a burgeoning multi-million dollar

Reuters/Shaun Best

Serena Williams

www.sportfiles.com

Venus Williams

Miss Lara Croft

genre known as anime and hentai. In Japanese, the word "hentai" means perversion. The word "anime" refers to a particular style of Japanese animation. This genre of animation utilizes digitally created women with exceptionally large eyes, wispy limbs, large breasts and curiously small mouths, formed to give the impression of both shock and innocence. (SEE PHOTO CREDITS OF ANIME ART)

Cultural influences can dominate biological predispositions, individual taste and other less robust cultural definitions of beauty. One case in point involves the now almost universal trend toward "thin as beautiful." The Western world's marketing of "thin" as ideal beauty has been dominant, even in the face of biological predispositions and long-standing cultural norms to the contrary. It is as though America's obsession with thin as ideal beauty is an omnipotent virus that, once introduced into new populations, immediately infects its host, and for which no cure exists. Twiggy was one of the first models who popularized the "gaunt" look. Twiggy made her appearance on the fashion scene in the 1960's, but her image lives on, as noted by the fact that "Twiggy" dolls are still being sold nearly a half-century later. The Franklin Mint, a purveyor of collectibles, marketed a Twiggy doll with the following ad copy: "She was a 17-year-old, 5-foot 7-inch, 91-pound girl from England named "Twiggy." (SEE PHOTO OF TWIGGY FROM *FRANKLIN MINT* AD) Of course, no discussion of exaggerated body proportions would be complete without mentioning the most popular doll ever: Barbie. If Barbie was a real person, she would stand 7' 2" tall; have a 40" bust, an 18" waist and 32" hips.

A study conducted by Dr. Anne Becker, a researcher at Harvard University, illustrates the importance of the media on body image. On the Pacific Island of Fiji, body image among young girls has changed since the introduction of television. In 1995, only 3 percent of Fiji's teenage girls reported vomiting to control their weight. By 1998, that figure had increased fivefold. Television, and the body images it brings viewers, was only widely introduced to Fiji in 1995. Up until that point, the Fiji high-volume diet of animal fat, yams, taro root, and cassava—and the body type it promotes—was for the most part accepted by teenage girls on the island. In 1998, Fiji had only one television station. What were some of the favorite TV shows on Fiji? Melrose Place, ER and Xena: Warrior Princess. Heather Locklear parading in your living room in syndication certainly doesn't promote an acceptance of one's "heavy" body type, especially if you are a teenage girl coming of age in Fiji. Of course, this effect is not exclusively the result of the introduction of television. Not only has television been introduced, but any number of media have made their way onto the island. All of those media, in one way or another, promotes a standard of beauty counter to what traditionally had constituted the cultural norm on Fiji.

China, too, is in the midst of cultural changes that may well rival Chairman Mao's Cultural Revolution. China has always been a country where a little extra weight meant health. Enter capitalism, circa early twenty-first century. Right there next to McDonalds and Dunkin Donuts one

This is the Classic Body Type in Anime/Hentai Drawings

The Franklin Mint's Commemorative Twiggy Doll
Sold in the Spring of 2001

finds a burgeoning weight loss industry. Elisabeth Rosenthal, of the New York Times News Service, reported her investigation of this new Chinese cultural revolution in an article which appeared in late 1999. The story chronicled changes in the Chinese ideal of beauty, which bears an uncanny similarity to the events which led to the cultural changes seen in Fiji. Rosenthal wrote about a Beijing psychiatrist named Dr. Zhang, who reported treating more and more patients with eating disorders. Dr. Zhang noted that "since China's opening and reform, the ideals and standards for so many things, including body type, have changed. Many people are paying more attention to self-improvement. The girls see the beauty contests and the ads for slimming drugs, and they absorb it all." Rosenthal cited the case of Teng Lue, a 16-year-old high school student in Beijing. Lue told Rosenthal that "Chinese girls think thinner is better, and fat kids are under a lot of pressure to reduce." Dr. Zhang told Rosenthal, "At 14 or 15, these kids get out into society and they begin to feel all sorts of pressures—these girls come in so underweight, and then they bring in advertisements for us to look at and argue that they don't have a problem." But have a problem they do. Ms. Rosenthal reported that cases of anorexia nervosa and bulimia, once virtually unknown in China, have multiplied exponentially in the last five years leading up to the millennium.

In a Los Angeles Times article, dated August 17, 2000, investigative journalist Ching-Ching Ni reported that numerous fat clinics and weight loss formulas have permeated the Chinese marketplace. Ni reported that 20% of Chinese people are considered overweight. Comparing that figure to the number of Americans who are rated as overweight, one must conclude that the burgeoning weight loss industry in China has room for capital appreciation. In the October 2002 issue of the Journal of the American Medical Association, researchers reported that 31 percent of adults in the United States are obese, up from 23 percent a decade ago. In 1980, that figure was 15 percent.

Lest one conclude that the burgeoning weight loss industry in China will actually impact that population's body type, one would do well to study California, perhaps the most body-conscious location in the United States. In the year 2000, the non-profit Public Health Institute, out of Berkeley, California, rated over half of Californians as officially overweight. Nevertheless, Californians are voracious consumers of diet and exercise programs and paraphernalia, as well as plastic surgery and cosmetics. It should also be obvious that California, in large part because of its indigenous entertainment industry, is a dominant force in defining what is and what is not beautiful for the rest of the world. Ironically, however, its own citizens appear to be losing a cultural battle defined in their own backyard.

Kids

Six million children are overweight in the United States. That number has doubled from 1980 to the year 2000, according to the Centers for Disease Control and Prevention. That same study found that 14 percent of all children ages 12 to 19 were seriously overweight. In addition to those numbers, another 25 percent or so of kids were found to be "chubby, but not "officially" obese. Medical researchers estimate that 21 percent of two-to five year-old children are either overweight or at serious risk of becoming overweight.

Ideal teen "image" as portrayed and sold by marketing moguls and their clients stand in stark contrast to the realities of real teen bodies. One of the problems that results for teens who do not possess the pop idol body is related to wardrobe. Where do "chubby" and obese teens find clothes to fit them? Kathy Boccella, a writer for the Knight Ridder News Service, interviewed Dr. Andy Tershakovec, the medical director of the weight-management program at Children's Hospital of Philadelphia. Dr. Tershakovec told Boccella that there exist three main issues that overweight teens must deal with. First, they must deal with teasing from other teens. Second, they must deal with limitations in physical activities, and third, overweight kids have trouble finding clothes that fit with the ideal teen image, yet still fit. These problems are most critical for teen girls.

According to Robert Atkinson, a spokesman for "Limited Too," a very desirous store for 10-year-olds, plus sizes make up about 12 to 15 percent of their catalogue business. Atkinson told Boccella that their plus size line debuted in the year 2000, because his store recognized that teen girls who happen to be overweight feel left out. He went on to say that it is all about fitting in. "Limited Too" jeans, which run $36.50 to $39.50 dollars a pair, cost $2 extra in larger sizes, which have an inch more room and are made of "flexible" material. Boccella researched other stores that are jumping on the plus size bandwagon. She found that Sears, which has sold "husky" sizes for years, has now been joined by "Land's End," "Hot Topic" and "Torrid," each a hot retailer in the teen market. Given how critical teens are when it comes to their own bodies, it is difficult to imagine that manufacturing stylish clothes in larger sizes will help anything except the store's bottom line.

Genes vs. Jeans

One of the most fascinating aspects of our culture's current definition of ideal beauty is that it is virtually always in conflict with one's gender based, ethnic and familial body inheritance. What this means, for example, is that the defined ideal of a narrow derriere, hips and thin thighs for women, just happens to coincide with the genetically programmed areas for concentrations of fat deposits. Thus, nature is forever battling the quest for culturally defined ideal hips, derrieres and thighs. That bio-cultural battle ensures an endless supply of diet gurus, potions, programs, elixirs, attitudes and paraphernalia that promise to defeat nature. The fact that the battle rages, and the profits are high, forces one to conclude that nature is winning the battle. The high profits and the marketing incentives they spawn suggest that the war is sure to continue.

It is not just fat deposits that define the battlefield. Take, for example, the nose. The most requested type of nose in all of plastic surgery is the petite and sculpted nose. It just so happens that millions upon millions of women inherit an anterograded nasal bridge, known as the humped or hooked nose. A similar number inherit a wide and flattened nasal tip: good for breathing, bad for the model's standard of beauty. The makeup industry and plastic surgeons benefit from this bio-cultural war over the shape of the human nose.

Changing one's body against its will results in ever more clever surgical techniques, as well as ever more clever beauty concoctions. It ensures the repeat customer for everything from makeup to plastic surgery. It also results in a new body type creation that is isolated from everything that identifies it as belonging to a unique person and genetic culture, because everybody who actually achieves the cultural definition of beauty begins to look the same. As a society, we are beginning to create, promote and accept the engineered look as the ideal.

The Engineered Look as the Ideal Image

Plastic surgeons have traditionally attempted to avoid what is termed the "operated on" look. The "operated on" look is characterized by a nose that is noticeably petite and sculpted; the skin around the eyes is drawn, the malar eminences (cheek bones) are enhanced, and the jaw area is characterized by "pulled-back" skin and underlying fascia: absent subcutaneous fat. Lips are made to be permanently pursed and artificially full. When referring to the breasts, the "operated on" breast possesses an overly defined perimeter with distended and relatively immobile tissue, along with a size that is often disproportionately large to the overall body frame dimension. In today's world, what we used to call the "operated on" look is becoming a cultural norm, if not a cultural ideal, within certain social strata. The "operated on" breast is often judged to be more attractive than the natural breast. The natural breast is not infrequently described by men as less attractive than the surgically altered breast because of its natural tendency to lose its shape when lying down and its proportionate size when compared to the rest of the body. A generation of men have grown up looking at nude women who have undergone breast augmentation surgery.

My own research has shown that over half of women who display their breasts within the context of their chosen profession have undergone breast enhancement surgery. Of those women who work in the various image professions, whether it be topless dancer or film actress, virtually all report that they have either had breast enhancement surgery or would consider such surgery at some point in the future. It is interesting to note that of those women who do possess natural breasts, virtually all of them do something to "enhance" their natural shape and form. The "pushup" bra, the underwire bra, and all of their various permutations, including the "wonder bra," modify the shape of the natural breast. In the beauty pageant business, the use of surgical tape to modify nearly perfect natural breasts is commonplace. The social dynamic set in play by the surgically altered breast devalues the natural breast, even the near perfect natural breast. The dynamic manifests when women who possess near perfectly shaped and sized breasts request breast augmentation surgery. It also manifests when men express a preference for the surgically altered breast.

When it comes to face lifts, a taut and wrinkle-free face, even if you are 75 years old, is more than an unnatural look. That same unnatural look connotes social prestige, wealth and position. Social gatherings of older women of affluence are often comprised of faces overly drawn and taut. My own research in the field of plastic surgery uncovered a trend in the latter part of the twentieth century for women sixty years and older to report dissatisfaction with the "refreshed look" face lift, favoring instead a face lift that prompted the question "When did you have the surgery?" as opposed to,"You look refreshed; what are you doing for yourself?"

Those who favor the "operated on" look can be identified by sociodemographic variables. Women over the age of sixty, with a yearly disposable income greater than $250,000, who live in upscale areas of the nation, and who frequent social gatherings for various and sundry philanthropic causes, favor the "operated on" look, especially when it comes to facelifts. The trend that I witnessed first-hand in the late 1980's occurred in La Jolla, California. I studied perceptions of the "operated on" look by sampling photographs from newspapers across the United States, with a particular focus upon the society page section of newspapers which covered the social activities of such geographic areas as Palm Beach, Florida, Beverly Hills, California, Palm Springs, California, Westchester County, New York, and the North Shore of Chicago, Illinois. Women from La Jolla, California, who met the sociodemographic fingerprint identified above, judged photographs taken from the various society sections of the sampled newspapers. These women rated as "very favorable" women who possessed the "operated on" look. On the other hand, women between the ages of 20 and 25, who were best described as struggling students, rated the same society page women as "very unfavorable." It is interesting to note that younger women who come from the same social strata as the society page older women, rated the "operated on" look as "favorable," just a slightly less favorable rating made by their older sociodemograhic matches. Thus, it appears that for affluent women who appear in the public arena, the "operated on" look is not only acceptable, but favored. Women who met the society page profile rated the overly drawn and taut face look more desirable when contrasted with a "refreshed look" face-lift. Middle-class women who had considered having surgery on their faces were evenly split between the "refreshed look" and the "operated on" look when it came to the look they favored.

Surgeons who have spent a lifetime perfecting their art find themselves in a quandary when their patients report dissatisfaction with the "refreshed look" facelift, favoring instead the look of an obvious facelift. I recall a patient from La Jolla who had undergone a complete facelift with a stunning result, a result that turned back the clock without any of the obvious signs of a surgical intervention. That patient showed up for her six-week postoperative exam with one of her friends. Both women were active in local social circles. The surgeon and I were proud of the surgical outcome, and frankly expected to hear numerous laudatory comments, including the fact that the patient's friend also wanted plastic surgery on her face, as well. Instead, what we heard was a polite, but nonetheless critical, review of the surgical outcome. "My friends have no idea that I have had work done. They just think that I look rested and better." The surgeon smiled and quietly said, "Thank you." At that point, our patient's friend asked whether or not the skin around her friend's eyes could be pulled back even more, and whether or not the skin around the jaw line could be made even more taut. I realized that what the women were describing was exactly what the surgeon had brilliantly avoided in his original surgery, and in so doing, had denied the patient from becoming a member of her social clique who had undergone a noticeable facelift. It is worth remembering that the physicians who perform the plastic surgery that we have come to recognize as the "operated on" look are, more often than not, among the most successful plastic surgeons in their particular geographical area. Often times these surgeons are among the best trained in the United States. That should not surprise the reader. After all, affluent women virtually always seek out those surgeons with the most famous clientele and successful practices who promise to make them beautiful. It is noteworthy that in all of my years of experience, I have never found a plastic surgeon to acknowledge, at least for public consumption, that he or she ever purposefully creates the "operated on" look. This denial is certainly supported by the patients of these same surgeons. Patients with the "operated on" look deny that their look is anything but a beautiful result. Given the denial of both patient and surgeon alike, one is left to wonder who is performing all of the obvious plastic surgery that is so easily recognized as the "operated on" look.

Chapter II: Makeup and Beauty

Cosmetics and makeup are a multi-billion dollar a year and growing international business. The following list of market study reports of this burgeoning worldwide business provides the reader with a sense of just how important beauty-care products are to commerce. What follows is a sampling of some of the market segments in the cosmetic industry: Lip Care; Lip Makeup; Medicated Skin Care; Toilet Soaps; Bath and Shower Care; Over–the-Counter Medicated Skin Care; Prescription Skin Care; Fragrances and Perfume; Hair Care; Oral Care; Shaving Men; Shaving Women; Deodorants; Facial Rejuvenation; Hair Colorants; Hair Perms; Feminine Hygiene; Nail Care; Eye Makeup; Face Depilatories; Body Depilatories; Grooming Aids (brushes, combs, etc.); Beauty Appliances (hair dryers, etc.); and a myriad of other items and products which promise an increase in beauty for the purchaser. What follows is a representative abstract for just one of these cosmetic and makeup market studies:

> "The worldwide lip care products market is a small part of the cosmetics and personal care (C&P) market. The lip care market is highly competitive and mirrors the trends in the C&P market. The report includes a brief profile of the product, and explores the factors that play an important role in influencing the market, which includes trends in pricing, packaging, distribution, emerging niches and technology advances. Regional market analysis, followed by strategic developments such as product launches licensing details, and others are also included. Primary markets worldwide are analyzed with annual estimates and projections. Geographic markets individually addressed are -The United States; Canada; Japan; Europe - France, Germany, Italy, the UK, Spain, Russia, Rest of Western Europe, Eastern Europe; Asia- Pacific, The Middle East and Latin America. Product segments separately analyzed include lip revitalizers, chap stick, lip medex, lip balms/ointments and lip shield." (Abstract from: Lip Care Products. Published by (GIA) is a U.S. based world leader in business intelligence and strategy support).

The price for such a report, as identified above, is $3,450. The cost is indicative of the value of this segment of the cosmetic industry.

Makeup is an over-the-counter solution to imperfections in beauty. Symmetry, a universally attractive feature, can be achieved by balancing asymmetries with dark and light shading. A crooked or asymmetrical nose is "straightened" by darkening the high points and lightening the low points. Foundations do a marvelous job of increasing both consistency of texture and color and can add an overall healthy "glow" to the skin.

Makeup can also accentuate that which is not flawed. Blush and lip color draw attention to areas of the face known to function as sexual cues. Makeup can function as pure adornment. For example, blush, eyeliner, and lipstick can be applied in excess. We might call this type of adornment party makeup. We can also add a special makeup adornment, such as glitter, false eyelashes or a penciled-in beauty mark.

Makeup tells others what we are up to. Most women reading this generally know what is meant by the terms "whore" makeup, "plain-Jane" makeup and "old lady" makeup. Makeup worn out of context is at best a faux pas, and at worst scandalous; for example: party makeup with glitter worn to a funeral.

Makeup provides a window into the universals of beauty. Everywhere in the world, women have always done something to enhance their lips, eyes and hair. The Egyptians institutionalized what we would call today beauty parlors. Hair color, nail polish and various emollients for the skin were not uncommon in ancient Egypt. Both men and women shaved their body hair. Egyptians used eyeliner in both matte and shiny textures. The makeup artists of the day knew about lead sulphide (galena) and lead carbonate (cerussite), two principal ingredients in Egyptian cosmetics. Models wearing green, blue and yellow eye liner and red lip color adorn the tombs of many a Pharaoh. (SEE ILLUSTRATIONS FROM EGYPT) Women have used iron ores, in various colors and shades, to color their faces for thousands of years. Henna was used to color hair in ancient Egypt, and many beauty supply stores in the modern world still carry henna-based products. Kohl, a lead-based eye color that was popular among ancient Egyptians, is still so prevalent in today's world that an alert was issued by the U.S. Customs Service in 1996, warning agents of Kohl's potentially toxic effects. (SEE CUSTOMS REPORT)

The spectrum of enhancements that women make to their lips ranges from placing saucer-type expanders in the lower lip to the rather ubiquitous custom of painting lips. The women of the Mursi tribe of Ethiopia begin expanding their lips as children. The size of the saucer-type expanders is the best predictor of how many head of cattle she will warrant in her dowry. The Kayapo of the Brazillian rain forest reserve such lip enhancements for the men of the tribe, where the size of the lips gives testament to the status of the particular tribesman.

Enhancements to the eye have ranged from merely coloring the area around the eye to the use of drugs which alters the size of the pupil. When altering eyes and lips, the tendency is to make them bigger and fuller. Such changes are not just about increasing visibility, but are designed to increase the amplitude of sexual cues to others. In the seventeenth century, some women would put the drug belladonna in their eyes. This drug relaxes ciliary muscles which control the size of the

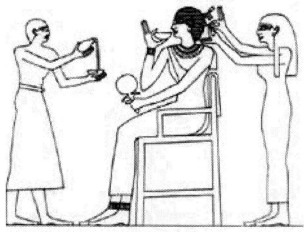

Egyptian Drawing Depicting a Beauty Salon   Egyptian Makeup Box

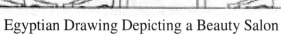

Stone Relief of an Egyptian Woman Applying Makeup

IA #53-15 - REVISED 1/26/96, IMPORT ALERT #53-15, "AUTOMATIC DETENTION OF
EYE AREA COSMETICS CONTAINING KOHL, KAJAL, OR ***SURMA***"

NOTE: This alert has been revised to add an additional name for the
product, create an attachment, and to update the format. Additional changes are
bracketed by asterisks (***).

TYPE OF ALERT: Automatic Detenti

***(Note: This import alert contains guidance to FDA field
personnel only. It does not establish any requirements or
create any rights or obligations on FDA or on regulated
entities.)***

PRODUCT: Any eye area cosmetic containing Kohl, Kajal, or ***Surma***

PRODUCT CODE: 53C[][][][]

PROBLEM: Unapproved Colors (UCNC)

PAC FOR
COLLECTION: 29002

COUNTRY: Germany (DE, 394)
                ***India (IN, 455)
                Pakistan (PK, 700)***

MANUFACTURER/
SHIPPER: See attachment

MANUFACTURER/
SHIPPER I.D.#:   See attachment

IMPORTER'S
I.D. #:   N/A

CHARGE: "The article is subject to refusal of admission pursuant to
                Section 801 (a)(3) in that it is not a hair dye and it appears
                to be, or to bear or contain, a color additive which is unsafe
                within the meaning of Section 721(a) [Adulteration, Section
                601(e)]."

If the product labeling states or suggests "FDA Approved," add
                a second charge:
 "The article is subject to refusal of admission pursuant to
                Section 801(a)(3) in that its labeling appears to be false or
                misleading [Misleading, section 403(a)]."

If the outer carton labeling (or immediate container labeling
                in cases where no outer carton exists) fails to bear an
                ingredient declaration, the following charge should be added:

The article is subject to refusal of admission pursuant to
                Section 801(a)(3) in that the label fails to bear an
                ingredient declaration in accordance with the requirements of
                Section 1454(c)(3)(B) of the Fair Packaging and Labeling Act
                and 21 CFR 701.3."

RECOMMENDING
OFFICE: DIOP (HFC-170)

REASON FOR
ALERT: This alert was ***first*** initiated in response to a report
                from the State of California, Department of Health Services,
                Food and Drug Branch, concerning the use of eye area cosmetic
                (e.g., pencils and eyeliners) containing Kohl and/or Kajal.
                These cosmetics were reportedly being imported from Germany
                and are labeled as having "FDA approval."

                ***A subsequent report received from the New York State
                Department of Health indicated that Surma, a powdered eye area
                product manufactured and used in Pakistan, India, and other
                Middle Eastern countries, was believed to be the source of
                lead poisoning in a young child. Available reference
                materials indicate that the Indian colorant "Surma" is also
                known in Arab countries as Kohl.

United States Customs Service' Warning Related to Kohl

pupil. The result was that these belladonna women would walk around with dilated pupils. Why did they do this? Because it made them more beautiful. Why did it make them more beautiful? Some researchers have argued that people possess a genetically wired-in attraction to large pupils. Researchers reason that when we like what we are looking at, our pupils naturally increase in size. As the object of someone's adoring attention we, in turn, find that person to be more attractive. Looking at someone who looks as though they are fascinated with us makes that person, in turn, more attractive. Like so much of our fascination with looks, our conscious understanding of this phenomenon is typically only as deep as reporting that we just think women with large pupils and larger-appearing eyes are pretty.

Our fascination with beauty can be very specific. In fact, our obsession with discrete areas of the face has spawned specialty niches in the beauty business, along with specific products, such as the eyebrow pencil. Here is just one example: Some salons are solely dedicated to eyebrow shaping. Some women have their eyebrows shaved off, and in their place, patrons have penciled-in the shape that best fits their mood or the current cultural standard of beauty. As of the writing of this book, one of the most popular looks at these specialty eyebrow salons derives from the movie stars of the 1940s and 50s, such as Audrey Hepburn, Ava Gardner and Elizabeth Taylor. (SEE PHOTOS OF AUDREY HEPBURN, AVA GARDNER AND ELIZABETH TAYLOR) These specialty salons are so busy that they typically have a waiting list.

The makeup armamentarium of the twenty-first century is a wonder to behold. In fact, so much can be done with state-of-the-art makeup that the person underneath all the products can remain not only hidden to the rest of the world, but to the wearer of the makeup as well. Makeup functions as a shared cue among women as to what constitutes beauty. As a result, we have style trends which define what one generation to the next looks like. Trends in the makeup business are not always dependent upon generation to generation changes, however. Whomever is in the public eye, and whomever has demonstrated some special attractiveness, can set a makeup trend.

For example, Monica Lewinsky, President Clinton's short-time paramour, set a lipstick trend in the spring of 1999, days after an interview with Barbara Walters which was watched by 30% of the homes in America. It is fascinating that her reputed love of oral sex with the President, and the makeup which adorned those same lips, would set a trend which prevented the manufacturer of her lipstick and lip liner (Club Monaco) from keeping product on retail shelves. This example highlights the powerful unconscious forces which are truly at work when it comes to beauty. If the unconscious could talk, it might argue that since Ms. Lewinsky is in the public spotlight, she must be desirable. Only beautiful people can be desirable, especially someone found to be attractive by such a powerful man as the President of the United States. Thus, celebrity often defines what constitutes beautiful makeup. The average person wants to share that special attractiveness. I want to look like the celebrity; therefore, I will adorn myself to look like the celebrity.

Some Famous Eyebrows

Ava Gardner

Audrey Hepburn

Elizabeth Taylor

The easiest way to do that is to emulate wardrobe and makeup. The logic is primitive and faulty, but logical in its error because beauty is so often identified with desire, and beauty is all about looks.

Tattoos

Tattooing, or body art, as some like to refer to it, has a long history dating back thousands and thousands of years, some believe as far back as the Upper Paleolithic Era (10,000-38,000 years ago). Makeup and the art of tattooing were contemporaneous practices among ancient cultures. The reader is referred to any number of works on the history of tattoos and tattooing, which is not the focus of this work. Our focus is on the relationship, or lack thereof, between tattoos and beauty.

Makeup is almost always designed to increase beauty, either through correction, enhancement or adornment; whereas tattooing is motivated by a number of often complex and interrelated social-psychological factors, most of which have nothing, per se, to do with beauty. Conscious and unconscious forces underlay the desire to tattoo one's body. What follows is a taxonomy of the various motivations and functions of the tattoo. Throughout history these motivations have remained constant, while cultural variations and trends have accentuated each at one time or another.

Membership

Tattoos have functioned as permanent marks on the human body which declared membership. A shared tattoo may show membership in a particular tribe or culture. Tattoos may also denote membership in subcultures, such as gangs, clubs and organizations. Seamen, for years, have consummated a right of passage in the Navy by having the ritual anchor tattooed onto their forearm.

Subsets of a particular culture are often denoted by tattoos which define very specific social roles. These tattoos are all different, but recognized as part of the same major cultural group. Referencing seamen again, they have at times used tattoos to denote rank and particular job duties. These are specified by the type of tattoo scarred onto their body. While each of these job, duty or rank tattoos are different, they are all recognized as denoting membership in the greater culture; that is, the Navy.

Ownership

Tattoos have an ignominious history of denoting ownership. Slaves were tattooed by their "owners," as were Jews catalogued by their Nazi captors. Couples involved in sado-masochistic relationships often denote ownership with tattoos. "Property of Jim" is just one example. This type of tattooing is akin to "branding."

Biocultural Landmarks

Tattoos can denote the transition from childhood to young adulthood. It can denote the transition to reproductive availability or the transition from adolescent to warrior. Puberty rites in some cultures include ritualized tattooing, often applied by elders in the tribe.

Pseudo-Military Stripes

Tattoos can function as a form of military stripe earned when its wearer has completed the tasks required to earn the stripe. For example, some gangs, when one of its members kills a rival gang member, denotes such an "accomplishment" with a stripe in the form of a tattoo.

Attitude

Tattoos can inform others of its owner's attitude about any number of issues and behavioral tendencies. The tattoo "T.R.O.U.B.L.E." suggests something about the mind-set of its wearer which motivated him or her to have such a word permanently scarred onto their body. A woman with a barbed wire tattoo may be communicating something about her attitude. "M.O.M." has tradition-ally been a tattoo associated with an attitude which has communicated betrayal from virtually everyone else in the world except mother.

The attitude motivation is one of the more interesting dynamics in the world of tattoos. The reader is left to ponder some of the following real life examples of attitude expressed by a tattoo: 1. A black widow spider tattooed onto the derriere of an attractive woman. 2. A "Crying Skull" tattooed onto the arm of a 16 year-old boy. 3. A snake image with fangs displayed tattooed onto the pubic area of a female grammar-school teacher. 4. A baby toting a machine gun tattooed onto the arm of a Hell's Angels member. (SEE PHOTO CREDITS OF TATTOOS WHICH EXPRESS ATTITUDE. Some of these tattoos, by the way, belong to celebrities. Can you guess which tattoos belong to Eminem, Britney Spears, JFK Jr, Barbie, Ozzy Osbourne? Answers can be found on our page of celebrity tattoos in this chapter)

Commitment

Tattoos may function as an expression of commitment to another person or group. When a lover's name or image is scarred onto one's body it may reflect either, and/or the wearer's need to show such commitment or the partner's need for such an expression of permanency in commitment and dedication. A tattoo of your partner's image and/or name declares a level of commitment that is a step up from the traditional wedding band.

Adornment

Tattoos may function as body art which is designed solely to increase attraction or attention

Various Examples of Tattoos that Express Attitude, Including Some that Belong to
Celebrities
(See Our Celebrity Tattoo Page for the Answers)

from others. When used this way, a tattoo is not unlike the dramatic use of makeup. Tattoos used primarily for adornment are usually aesthetically pretty. In addition, the subject matter is typically of a beautiful object, for example, a rose.

Antisocial Expression

Tattoos may function as a "thumbing of the nose" to mainstream society. The subject matter of the tattoo, when used in this way, is generally designed purposely to offend mainstream or conservative sensibilities. By definition, the owner of this type of tattoo relies upon the presence of a culture which considers his or her tattoo to be an expression of an antisocial attitude. In some parts of the world, the mere existence of a tattoo suffices to express an antisocial intent. In other cultural enclaves, such as Greenwich Village or Hollywood, one must rely upon a particularly offensive subject matter if the owner is to be successful at an antisocial expression, since tattoos are "mainstream" within those particular cultural enclaves.

A question of some interest involves whether or not the expression of an antisocial attitude to get a tattoo is merely that, a symbolic expression, or whether getting a tattoo for some people can predict other maladaptive behaviors, as well. In June of 2002, a research article appeared in the journal *Pediatrics*. The researchers looked at younger people between the ages of 12 to 22 years of age. Compared to young people without tattoos and/or body piercings (other than earring piercings), the group with tattoos and/or body piercings were twice as likely to engage in sexual activity and use so-called "gateway drugs" like marijuana, alcohol and cigarettes. The tattoo and piercing groups were three times more likely to use hard drugs such as Ecstasy, cocaine and methamphetamines. Both males and females with tattoos were more violent, as measured by their tendency to get into a fist fight. Females with tattoos or piercings were found to think more about suicide.

Look at Me

This motive is so rudimentary that it is often overlooked. Some people simply want to be looked at, and they feel having a tattoo that is either pretty, provocative or just there, will achieve their goal. Some people feel that tattoos provide a starting point for the initial interaction with a stranger, i.e., the tattoo becomes a conversation piece. As tattoos become more commonplace, especially among young women, the tattoo may lose some of its attention-getting qualities.

Tattoo-Culture

Some tattoos are made as part of the tattoo culture, wherein simply having multiple tattoos, elaborate tattoos or very expensive or special tattoos, is for other tattoo connoisseurs. The animated tattoo, that is, a tattoo located onto a moving body area or part, is often created for the pleasure of other tattoo connoisseurs.

The above referenced motives and purposes of tattoos are not mutually exclusive with one another. Multiple motives to scar one's body with a tattoo are commonplace. Furthermore, even if the wearer of a tattoo is purely interested in self-adornment, he or she may inadvertently be assumed by others to have made an antisocial statement, have made themselves sexually available or any number of unintended effects.

Regardless of the motive(s) to have a tattoo, the gravity of a tattoo derives in part from the fact that a tattoo is thought of as permanent. When Tom Arnold tattooed a portrait of his former wife Roseanne on his chest, the act of having the tattoo garnered its significance, in large measure, from the fact that Roseanne's face will always be with him. (SEE PHOTOS OF CELEBRITY TATTOOS) As stated earlier, a tattoo utilized this way, is an expression of commitment that makes the wedding band pale in comparison. In addition to the permanency of a tattoo, the act of scarring one's body with ink is painful. Thus, paired with the permanency aspect of the tattoo, pain increases the level of commitment and seriousness of the desire to express one's motive(s).

Health Risk Issues

The act of having a tattoo scarred onto one's body can be very dangerous. The American Red Cross, in recognition of the health risks associated with getting a tattoo, screens blood donors on this very issue. Prospective donors who have had been tattooed within the last 12 months are not allowed to donate blood. In March of 2002, Pamela Anderson-Lee told CNN that she became Hepatitis-C positive when she shared a tattoo needle with her former husband, Tommy Lee. (SEE PHOTO CREDIT OF PAMELA ANDERSON-LEE)

Legal Issues

The reader might find it interesting to note that the act of getting a tattoo is not legal everywhere in the United States. As of the writing of this book, Oklahoma and South Carolina have outlawed the practice of tattooing. Not uncommonly, opponents of tattooing cite health reasons for their opposition to this ancient practice. Long before Pamela Anderson-Lee went public with her case of hepatitis, an outbreak of that disease in the 1960s on Coney Island raised lawmakers' concerns. But as we have already seen, the act of tattooing is often influenced by any number of complex social and psychological, and yes, legal issues.

In 1999, a tattoo artist by the name of Ronald White violated South Carolina's prohibition against the act of tattooing. He was prosecuted, and as far as sentences go in South Carolina, Mr. White got off easy with a criminal conviction of five years probation and a fine. But this case did not end there. Mr. White took his case all the way to the United States Supreme Court, in an effort to appeal from a South Carolina State Supreme Court ruling which upheld Mr. White's lower court conviction. On October 7, 2002, the Supreme Court refused to hear his case, thereby affirming his

Celebrity Tattoos Representing Various Motivations

Tom Arnold

Angelina Jolie

Cher

Pamela Anderson-Lee

Answers from Page 41

A.	Anonymous	E.	Barbie
B.	Anonymous	F.	Eminem
C.	Ozzy Osbourne	G.	JFK Jr. (dagger)
D.	Anonymous	H.	Britney Spears

conviction. At issue was whether or not the practice of tattooing is a form of religious or political speech protected by the Constitution of the United States. As the legal scholar Jonathan Turley has observed about the South Carolina State Supreme Court's ruling: "For its part, the South Carolina Supreme Court held that, though a tattoo might be a form of protected expression, the 'process' of tattooing was not protected. This is akin to treating the Declaration of Independence as protected speech but not Benjamin Franklin's printing of the document."

Location

Where a tattoo is placed further adds to its meaning. One of the most interesting placements is what I call the "peek-a-boo" or "tease" placement. Women are the purchasers of most peek-a-boo tattoos. Often this tattoo is placed so that it will "peek" just above the belt-line, or it may be placed just slightly below the panty-line, such that a portion of it remains visible. Another popular location is the small of the back, where part of the tattoo peeks above the belt line only to tease the viewer about what may be below. The breast and derriere cleavage are also popular areas upon which women place the teasing tattoo. Such a tattoo is both a tease and an expression of holding back on the part of the wearer.

One of the more interesting placements for a tattoo is the hidden placement. Genitalia or proximal placements are reserved for "special viewing." Under the arm placement, though relatively rare, requires a movement to make the tattoo visible. Both "peek-a-boo" and "special viewing" tattoos are crystal clear metaphors of feminine ambivalence and selectivity when it comes to expressions of coital sexuality.

I'm Special

The final motive to have a tattoo is particularly important to our focus here because of its relationship to beauty. Studies in the United States have shown that the typical consumer for tattoos, as we enter the new millennium, is a female between the ages of 18 and 30. During the decade of the 1990s, according to U.S. News and World Report, tattoo parlors made up the sixth-fastest growing retail business in the United States. The single fastest growing demographic group patronizing tattoo parlors is the white middle-class female suburbanite.

The increasing popularity of tattoos, among women who are at the peak of their physical attractiveness, is a manifestation of the intense competition between women which encourages them to try anything in order to garner attention and to feel special. Being pretty and sexy simply isn't enough in today's world to feel special and unique. The "I'm Special" motive to get a tattoo is really an expression of feeling lost in a sea of homogenization. The homogenization of women's looks and personalities has encouraged women to look to artificial means by which she may become unique and different from her peers. The reader is referred to our chapter entitled *The Cult of*

Some Examples of Washable Tattoos from *Body Graphics*

the Beautiful Egg for a further explication of the "I'm Special" motive to get a tattoo. (SEE PHOTO CREDITS OF VARIOUS EXAMPLES OF TATTOOS)

Permanent Makeup

Tattoos, in the form of permanent makeup, are a distinctly different class of body art. Eyeliner helps to highlight the eye, which appears to be a biologically based determinant of beauty. Thus, permanent makeup shares virtually none of the psychosocial characteristics which define the meanings behind a tattoo, though technically the same tattooing process is used for both. Tattooing a little red devil onto the breast is purely psychosocial in its motivation and purpose, whereas permanent eyeliner is merely a smudge free form of makeup and is most often motivated by a desire for convenience.

Makeup is all about beauty. Tattoos are about man's relationship to his culture, his group and his desire to express himself to others. Tattoos may be beautiful, their owner may not be. Beautiful makeup virtually always makes its wearer more attractive. Sometimes a tattoo makes its owner hideous, which quite ironically may be exactly what motivated having the tattoo in the first place.

Makeup Magic

And finally, I have decided to include just a few illustrations of how makeup changes our perception of beauty. The photographs on the next few pages are of beautiful women, with and without makeup. It just so happens that most of us never get to see these beautiful women without their makeup. I'll leave it up to the reader to ponder their own emotional reaction to these photographs, and what that reaction means with regard to the importance of makeup on our perceptions of beauty. To be perfectly accurate, the differences that you will notice are not only related to makeup, but also to hair style, lighting, camera angle and lens, in addition to facial expression. Nevertheless, makeup, or its absence, plays a significant part in the differences you will notice in our celebrity photos.

Courtney Cox

Christina Applegate

Ellen Degeneres

 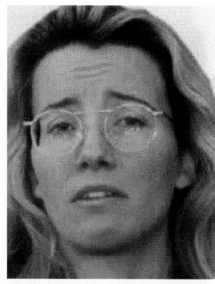

Emma Thompson

Pamela Anderson

Madonna

Britney Spears

Selected Photographs from: ebaumsworld.com

Christina Aguilera

Jennifer Lopez

Chapter III: Rich Man/Pretty Woman

In my professional life, I have spent a great deal of time around powerful men and beautiful women. One thing you learn early on is that the two go together. One or the other of these two groups have been my clients, my patients, my research subjects and my friends. Studies have shown that as the attractiveness of the girlfriend or wife increases, so does the income of her boyfriend or husband. Another thing you learn from experience is that the beautiful women in these rich man/pretty woman relationships will, sooner or later, become very unhappy.

My rich male clients are fond of telling the story about the three friends in a bar who notice the entrance of an absolutely stunning and beautiful woman. One friend points her out and exclaims: "Somewhere, someone is tired of that." The first time I heard that story I knew something profound was behind using the word "that" rather than "her" to refer to the woman.

To understand the rich man/pretty woman-"that" connection, you first have to understand that beautiful women begin life as pretty girls. Study after study has shown that pretty little girls are treated differently. That treatment is almost always positive from little boys and men alike. That treatment isn't always so predictably positive when it comes from other women or little girls, however.

A lifelong pattern of being the girl other girls love to hate begins as early as kindergarten. One of my little attractive female research subjects, age 5, had her hair spray-painted by two 7-year-old female students. I took it upon myself to investigate who these rogue spray painters might be. They turned out to be average-looking little girls with brown hair. After some clinical probing it became obvious that my little research subject's only sin was that she had been born beautiful, and that was enough to warrant the assault from the jealous girls.

One thing is for certain: as soon as the pretty little girl is seen by little boys, she gets attention. She learns that she has something that all the boys seem to like, and like a lot. Studies of seven year-old pretty girls find that their male classmates have already learned to shower them with gifts. The pretty girls at this age have already learned that they are entitled to have it their way, except from other little girls. Those "other" little girls learn a painful lesson that the gifts and attention showered upon pretty girls are denied them.

Childhood beauty affects not only relationships at school, but the family environment as well. Daddy's little princess is all the more regal if she is pretty. Rampant competition between pretty little girls and their mothers for daddy's attention is legend, and has been documented in my own research involving beauty pageant contestants.

"It"

Pretty little girls make a logical mistake when it comes to interpreting the meaning of the attention they receive, a mistake that accompanies the pretty little girl into womanhood. The primary mistake is that she thinks that boys and men are attracted to her, not her beauty. Suzy, Anastasia, Lisa, or all the other pretty girl names, think that Johnny is looking at them, when in reality he is looking at "it." This mistake creates an unjustified sense of confidence and often arrogance on the part of the pretty girl/beautiful woman that is inevitably set straight sooner or later. The men in the bar were profoundly and painfully insightful when they referred to the woman as a "that", not a "her."

Men, unless taught otherwise, may well have a tendency to objectify women, due in part to the fact that relating to a person is always more complex than relating to a more uni-dimensional entity. But when it comes to beautiful women, even men who strive to have a meaningful relationship with them often find themselves relating to the "beauty" and not the person. Beautiful women experience this all-too-familiar pattern of objectification as impersonal and universally unpleasant. This objectification phenomenon is taken personally, in the same way that attention from men is taken personally. Both objectification and attention are impersonal and are related to beauty itself, not the possessor of "it."

A beautiful woman or pretty girl finds it almost impossible to fully comprehend that the attention she receives, and all that goes with it, has little or nothing to do with who she is, absent her beauty. The fact that virtually all of the attention and much of the material benefits she receives from men, however, does not mean that there is not a wonderful person beneath the beauty. But this person beneath the beauty, unfortunately, is all too frequently influenced by the attention "it" receives. In virtually every high school across America we find beautiful girls who have developed a false sense of their own importance. They get attention from teachers, from peers, from construction workers, from young and old alike. This attention, and the gifts and favors it buys, helps to create a sense of entitlement, arrogance, self-absorption and dismissive callousness toward anyone who does not fit in with their immediate desires.

Self-absorbed beauty seldom goes unpunished in the real world. Failing to distinguish between being an "it" and a "me" typically arrests inner development. Personal resiliency and long-term self worth are never allowed to fully develop. Time is the enemy. Men "get used to" beauty over time. Once men know how to get beautiful women, they find an ample supply of them waiting to replace the "it" who came before her.

Wealthy Men and the Women Who Marry Them

In studying the wealthiest men in the world, not one of them was judged to be handsome by independent raters. In fact, the vast majority of wealthy men were judged to be unattractive, rather than just "average" looking. Handsome is not a moniker the vast majority of rich men heard as they were growing up. (SEE PHOTO CREDITS OF WORLD'S RICHEST MEN) Every little boy learns early on that pretty girls are attracted to the "cute" boy. Beauty, or the absence of it, to be precise, is what helps to motivate unpopular little boys to become rich and powerful.

A full page ad in a large Southern California newspaper captured this phenomenon in an advertisement for a computer company in the Spring of 1998. The ad included a photo of a young man, probably in his teens. The boy had an awkward look which included some rather thick glasses. The ad read: "Remember the geek from junior high who used to try and buy your friendship? He is still trying to buy it." (SEE PHOTO CREDIT OF COMPUTER AD). The ad went on to tout just how far this unattractive young man was willing to discount his computers just to be liked. The content of this particular ad highlighted the compensatory mechanism that so many unattractive boys adopt in their life. The boy in the ad was going to make up for his unattractiveness by offering a great deal on a computer.

This compensatory mechanism often becomes imbedded in the psyche of the unattractive boy. And for those young men thought of as "geeks" who finally achieve material wealth and/or fame, the ultimate compensatory act is to acquire beauty. The one thing the boy in the ad will buy, that will mean the most to him when he has lots of money from selling his discounted computers, is the pretty little girl he wanted as a child. This is the same pretty little girl who, before he became rich, at best patronized him, and at worst rejected him and most likely simply ignored him.

In yet another ad in a large Southern California newspaper which appeared in the Spring of 2002, a national advertiser for a satellite television service showed the photographs of two young men side by side. On the left we see Frank, and on the right we see Eugene. (SEE PHOTO CREDIT OF "FRANK AND EUGENE" AD) Frank, a noticeably more attractive person than Eugene, has a caption under his picture which states that he has received a lot of perks for free. Under Eugene's picture we read the cryptic and patronizing words: "Someone, please tell Eugene he can get it too."

Unattractive little boys are often ignored, rejected or patronized in the national media. Of course, pretty girls do the same, but not with the same conscious disregard used by advertisers. Pretty girls have no idea that when they enter a public place they are displaying their beauty for all to see. Pretty girls, however, are extremely selective about whom they will allow to approach them. From the unattractive boy's perspective, he is being solicited by the girl's beauty, only to be rejected when he approaches. It is as though someone calls out to you to "come here," only to then tell you to go away once you approach.

The unpopularity of unattractive little boys is a big part of their drive to excel in other areas,

Top Ten Wealthiest Men of All Time
Dollar Values are Represented in 2001 dollars

10. Sheikh Zayed Bin Sultan Al Nahyan -- $ 23 billion
The United Arab Emirates Sheikh has considerable holdings in oil,
property and various investments.

9. Paul Allen -- $25 billion
Microsoft co-founder and Vulcan Ventures founder.

8. Warren Buffett -- $28 billion
The"Oracle of Omaha" and president of Berkshire Hathaway.

7. King Fahd Bin Abdul Aziz Alsaud -- $30 billion
In power since 1982, the 77-year-old Saudi Arabian
King's fortune has swollen in recent years.

6. Lawrence J. Ellison -- $55 billion
Oracle's Chief Executive Officer.

Source: Dennis O'Connell
Entertainment Correspondent - *AskMen.Com*

Top Ten Wealthiest Men of All Time
Dollar Values are Represented in 2001 dollars

5. William Gates III -- $60 billion
Currently the world's richest man, at one point, Gates'
fortune was creeping towards the $100 billion mark.

4. John Jacob Astor (1763-1848) -- $85 billion
Adjusted for time, Astor, "the Self-Made Money-Making
Machine's" fortune would rank at roughly $85 billion in 2001.

3. Cornelius Vanderbilt (1794-1877) -- $100 billion
An American steamship and railroad builder, financier, promoter,
and executive, Vanderbilt left an estate of roughly $100 million,
which, in 2001 dollars, represents an astonishing $100 billion.

2. Andrew Carnegie (1835-1919) -- $110 billion
By the time he passed away in 1919, Carnegie had given away
over $350 million. In 2001 dollars he would be worth $110 billion.

1. John D. Rockefeller (1839-1937) -- $200 billion
The man who has a Center named after him in New York, he
built, dominated, controlled, and ultimately lost the Standard Oil
Company.

Source: Dennis O'Connell
Entertainment Correspondent - *AskMen.Com*

Some Other Very Wealthy Men

Michael Dell -- $20 billion

Steve Ballmer, Microsoft -- $19.5 billion

Phillip Anschutz -- $15.5 billion

Rupert Murdoch -- $5.3 billion

He's still trying to buy your love.

Advertisement from the *San Diego Union,* May 6, 1998

Frank gets it
Free for 3 Months, day and night, all over
the house and in all kinds of entertaining ways.

Someone, please tell Eugene he can
get it too.

Frank and Eugene Promotion
with Advertsing Copy

most notably, the quest for money and power. Nevertheless, even if the unattractive little boy achieves wealth and power as an adult, the hostility he harbors toward pretty girls, the product of years of sexual rejection, cannot be underestimated and never completely goes away. That hostility is ultimately directed at the pretty woman for any number of her unforgivable sins committed as a pretty girl. It is also directed at the boy who received the attention from the pretty little girl.

How is it that pretty women end up with rich powerful men? Pretty girls believe that they should have everything nice. In the jargon of clinical psychology, this is called entitlement. Material items, privilege and the lifestyle which goes along with it, takes money. It would be easy to conclude that pretty girls are primarily motivated by material greed. Such is not the case. Attaining material wealth, and/or associating with a man with power and prestige, becomes a validation of a pretty girl's beauty. The prettier you are, the more nice things and privileges you should have. If she doesn't already have a privileged lifestyle, then she finds a man who will buy it for her. Having your own material wealth, as in the case of successful models or movie stars, does not fulfill the need to validate self through association with money, power and prestige.

There seems to be little doubt that beautiful women seek out men with money. Similarly, men with money feel entitled to have beautiful women. Acquiring a "trophy" wife or girlfriend is quite common for men of wealth. Research validates the tendency for this union to take place. As previously mentioned, one of the best predictors of a man's income is the beauty of his wife or girlfriend. The more money he makes, the prettier his wife or girlfriend is likely to be.

In February of 2000, Fox broadcast a show entitled: "Who Wants to Marry a Multi-Millionaire?" During the first half hour of the two-hour program, 12.3 million viewers watched. In the second half hour that figure jumped to 18.9 million, with the final hour of the show garnering an astounding 22.8 million viewers.

The show featured a virtual bevy of beautiful women who competed for their multi-millionaire husband–to-be, about whom the contestants knew nothing except that he was rich. The winner actually married the multi-millionaire on air. Darva Conger, an attractive emergency room nurse from Santa Monica, married Rick Rockwell, a former comedian turned real-estate investor from San Diego. Within weeks, Ms. Conger had the marriage annulled, and within one year she was on the cover of Playboy magazine. (SEE PHOTOS OF DARVA CONGER)

Ms. Conger and Mr. Rockwell became instant celebrities after the airing of the program. Ms. Conger, in particular, made countless radio and television appearances. Likewise, virtually all of the other contestants made the press circuit as well. Remarkably, each and every contestant, particularly Ms. Conger, emphatically denied that money had anything to do with her willingness to participate in a contest where the winner, by design, was required to marry a man about whom she knew nothing except that he was rich. Darva was recognized for her beauty, and Mr. Rockwell found himself subjected to often times cruel commentary in the media, which focused in large

(top) Darva Conger Kisses Rick Rockwell On-Stage After Winning
Who Wants to Marry a Multi-Millionaire?
(lower right) Darva Conger Being Interviewed After She Divorced Rick Rockwell

Darva Conger on the Cover of *Playboy Magazine*

Photo by Randall Michelson

Darva Conger (left) with Hugh Hefner

measure on his appearance. The universal denial on the part of the contestants that money had anything to do with their choice to participate in the program, along with Mr. Rockwell's denial, albeit less dogmatic, that Ms. Conger's beauty was the driving force behind his selection of her as his bride, illustrates the strength of the various psychological defenses at work in the rich man/ pretty woman relationship.

I have included a couple of comic strips which illustrate two of the most common dynamics at work when it comes to beauty, wealth and the defenses which protect our collective awareness of the rich man/pretty woman relationship. Wiley Miller, the author of a comic strip entitled "Non Sequitur," highlighted that part of our culture which conditions young girls to the notion of finding a rich man. (SEE PHOTO CREDIT OF "NON SEQUITUR" COMIC STRIP) Jerry Scott and Jim Borgman, the authors of the comic strip "Zits," came up with a story that illustrates the conse- quences that await men who are candid about their love of beauty. (SEE PHOTO CREDIT OF "ZITS" COMIC STRIP)

Despite the fact that the pretty girl turned beautiful woman may now allow the rich man, former rejected boy, to approach her, even sleep with her, it doesn't mean that she accepts, or even likes him. Some beautiful women play the role better than others. Unfortunately, in many instances, the rich man may be with a beautiful woman, but he doesn't "have" her. Rich men are not oblivious to the tenuous nature of their relationship with beauty, and many become pathologically jealous. It just so happens that the rich man is exquisitely sensitive to rejection; after all, he has had a lifetime of practice at the hands of attractive females. Moreover, rich men never quite rid themselves of the resentment and insecurities they developed because of the rejection they experienced while grow- ing up.

When beauty does leave the rich man, she often leaves him for an even richer man. Mark Hughes, the late multi-millionaire who started the business known as Herbalife, married four beauty queens, the last being Darcy LaPier-Hughes (SEE PHOTO CREDITS OF DARCY LAPIER HUGHES AND SUZAN HUGHES). The widow Hughes' nuptial provenance provides a classic illustration of the rich man/pretty woman connection. In the summer of 2000, Darcy gave an inter- view to the British magazine "Hello." In that interview, she gave voice to what now should be recognized as a template for ambitious pretty girls everywhere. Darcy told the interviewer, "I was interested in science, but my girlfriends soon discovered the power of using the right lipstick, and when I looked at myself in the mirror one day, I thought, 'Hey, I'm pretty good-looking!'" This quote came from a high-school dropout who, reportedly, is the only child of Native American parents. Before Darcy discovered how to parlay her looks into millions by hooking up with rich men, she worked in a number of low-paying jobs on the outskirts of Portland, Oregon. Reportedly, one of those jobs found the future beauty queen, wife of millionaires, catching chickens so that they could be slaughtered.

Excerpt from the Comic Strip *Non Sequitur*
by Wiley Miller

Jerry Scott and Jim Borgman's Comic Strip *Zits*

Darcy LaPier-Robertson-Rice-Van Damme-Hughes

...ity of Angles
BY ANN O'NEILL

...an Hughes maintains that ...orporate positions place the ...in conflict of interest. Her ...aims the value of the estate, ...stimated at $350 million, has ...lied through mismanage- ...She also claims the trustees ...d their duty through "their ...sty to Alex and his mother." ...example, she cites their re- ...to turn over a go-cart and ...s' favorite shirt to his son.

...trustees insist they were ...nally appointed by Mark ...s, while trust documents ex- ...y excluded Suzan Hughes ...ny rights to or control of the

...zan Hughes was engaged in ...l battle with Mark Hughes ...he day that he told her he ...ing for divorce until the day ...d," Klein said. "This lawsuit ...thing more than a thinly ...attempt to obtain what she ...nable to in her prenuptial ...nent, divorce settlement or ...sequent letters, threats and ...s while Mark Hughes was

...k Hughes died a year ago of ...al combination of alcohol ...n antidepressant. His estate ...s about 13 million shares of ...life common stock.

LAWSUIT: Suzan Hughes wants a bigger chunk of the Herbalife founder's estate for her son.

Michelson Celebrity Archive

Suzan Hughes, Second Wife of the Late President of *Herbal Life,* Mark Hughes; Also a Former *Hawaiian Tropic Beauty Queen*

Darcy's first marriage was to a non-millionaire, her long-time friend Larry Ray Robertson. But that marriage was doomed once she won the 1986 Oregon Miss Hawaiian Tropic title. It was during that beauty pageant that Darcy caught the eye of Ron Rice, the founder and multi-million-aire owner of Hawaiian Tropic Suntan Oil. (SEE PHOTO CREDITOF RON RICE) One thing led to another and in 1990 Darcy gave birth to the Suntan Oil magnate's child. Soon after that, Darcy married her first multi-millionaire in 1990. It didn't take long for the bloom to fall off her first rich man/pretty woman relationship, however. Reportedly, the couple drifted apart over the next two years after their marriage. According to Rice, he suspected that Darcy was having an affair with the action movie star Jean-Claude Van Damme. Regardless of the truth of that allegation, it is a fact that in 1994, Darcy married her second multi-millionaire husband, Jean-Claude Van Damme. During the next few years of their marriage, the couple reportedly filed for divorce four times.

According to court documents, Darcy accused Jean-Claude of beating her and using her in lurid sex games. Shortly after the last court documents had been filed, Darcy had a blind date with her soon-to-be-third multi-millionaire husband, Mark Hughes. They married on Valentine's Day in 1999, after a year-long courtship. Reportedly, Hughes had drawn up a prenuptial agreement which promised his pretty wife one million dollars at every wedding anniversary during the first five years of their marriage, an extra $25,000 annually after six years, and 10 million cash at his death.

As a former Judge of two regional Hawaiian Tropic Beauty Pageants, I can say with some personal experience that many of the contestants share Darcy's intuitive sense of how their looks can be parlayed into material wealth. Male judges at these events are often chosen because of their relatively high-profile jobs, which often means that they have money. I have judged these pageants with media types, sports stars and business men. Time and time again we see the pattern, where the very successful beauty pageant contestant trades her beauty pedigree for marriage. For example, the former Miss Universe, Cecilia Bolocco, married millionaire and past Argentinian President, Carlos Menem. When the two married in May of 2001, the former Miss Universe was 36 years old—and the former President was 70.

Sports stars, financial barons and sometimes even very smart men are targeted by the beautiful woman. This is because these socially desirable men validate her beauty. Beautiful women feel they are entitled to a special man, a man who can buy them the material items which are part of her birthright. Whomever society defines as "special men" becomes the group from which the beautiful woman selects her self-validating man.

When the beautiful woman truly falls in love, it is often with a man whom they feel can put her in her place. In other words, a man who is not overwhelmed by her beauty. This behavior begs the question: why are beautiful women attracted to this kind of man? Beautiful women are not masochistic by nature. Nonetheless, they yearn for a man who doesn't value what ultimately de-

Photo Courtesy of Premier Media Group

Ron Rice, President of *Hawaiian Tropic* with Unnamed Model

fines her—her physical attractiveness. A man who can put her in her place, by definition, doesn't fall under her beautiful spell. Knowing all too well the power of her beauty, she can only conclude that any man who can do without her beauty must be powerful indeed. Thus, the man who doesn't fall under her spell, and who really doesn't care one way or the other about having her, is the one she can't live without. He is the one more powerful than she. It may be the guitar teacher or the husband of another woman, but it is he whom she is really attracted to. Alas, the pattern of rich man/pretty woman repeats itself with often tragic predictability. The childhood trauma for the unattractive millionaire boy repeats itself when beauty distances herself, the pretty girl is finally put in her place by the one she can't live without, and all live unhappily ever after.

Sports Stars

One particular rich man/pretty woman match-up deserves special attention. This match-up occurs when the pretty woman becomes involved with a sports star. Go to the most expensive ski resorts, vacation destinations, rich neighborhoods, and especially sporting events, and you will see scores and scores of attractive women, many of whom look very much alike. Look in the "wife and girlfriend" section of bleachers or sidelines at a sporting event, and you'll immediately see living proof of this mirror image phenomenon. (SEE RYDER CUP PHOTO)

This particular match-up, however, is not infrequently characterized by stressful relationships. Study after study of the incidence of rape, assault and abuse target high school, college and professional male athletes as high-risk dates and husbands. For example, on July 9, 1999, University of Minnesota investigators reported 40 incidents of alleged sexual assault and domestic abuse by student athletes. To make matters worse, the report cited several examples of an often repeated pattern recognized by its "favoritism toward student athletes and insensitivity toward female victims, on the part of university officials." That is just one university in one state. One interesting website, which was active as of the fall of 2003, is **www.cracksmoker.com/MLB1.htm.** This site chronicles various legal difficulties, not just those involving drugs, as reported in the press, involving major league baseball players. A cursory review of those reports from this website illustrates some of the reported problems these athletes have with their girlfriends and spouses.

Beautiful women seldom take these and similar affronts to their status in life lying down. A common response is to try and destroy the sport star's public image. Contentious divorces and a plethora of tell-all books about how the sports hero is not really a hero after all are really nothing more than the heat given off from the deadly mix of beauty and sports star. Once again, beauty ends up unhappy.

The Wives and Girlfriends of the 1999 American Ryder Cup Team (From the Opening Day Ceremonies of the 1999 Ryder Cup, Brookline, Massachusetts)

(Below) Question and Answer from Walter Scott's "Personality Parade" in Parade Magazine (June 23, 2002)

Q Golf star Tiger Woods' recent girlfriends, Joanna Jagoda and Elin Nordegren, look alike. Why does he always date beautiful, tall blondes?—Nicole R., Baton Rouge, La.

A Because he can.

Tiger Woods and His Former Girlfriend Joanna Jagoda

Allsport Photo
From the 1999 Ryder Cup Brookline, Massachusettes

71

Male Justification

Men who lust after beautiful women at the expense of others in their life virtually always justify their behavior by pointing out that it is "natural," and "it is just the way men are." What is often missed, however, is that the male contribution to this psychodrama can and often does have unbelievably lethal consequences. Machismo, dominance behaviors, symbolic sexual prowess and gender bias and oppression—all have their roots in the male's obsession with how beautiful women enhance his ego.

Men often intertwine their professional identities with their obsession with beautiful women. The trophy wife or girlfriend is testimony to the rich man's success in his chosen profession. Men are quite good at denying the fact that without material wealth, the would-be trophy wife or good-looking girlfriend would not give them the time of day. Trophy women deny the fact that their husbands or boyfriends may not like them. In fact, he may even hate them. They are, after all, when all is said and done, just another designer golf club in his golf bag that he shows off to his friends. Trophy women who seek out men are the material by-product of a self-fulfilling prophecy that is secondary to a society created by men where materialism, power, dominance, wealth and beautiful women are synonymous with having achieved alpha-male status.

The sexual realities associated with men who own trophy wives undermine the machismo myth: enter Viagra. For years, trophy wives and girlfriends could allow their machismo-puffing partners to parade them around before their peers in public. But once behind closed doors, the relief afforded by reduced or absent sexual intercourse made the relationship at least tolerable. Viagra has changed all of that. Anecdotal evidence is beginning to appear that suggests that trophy wives and girlfriends are thinking twice about their role, in part because there is no longer a safe harbor back home.

Viagra is also beginning to affect men and their defenses. It is appreciably harder to deny what truly binds his beautiful young mate to him when she must work hard to pretend to enjoy intimacy. The stress on both partners has increased, to the point where the myth is harder to maintain in the mind of the man and the role of trophy wife has become almost intolerable. The truth of what brings these two genre of people together bleeds through an ever-thinning set of defenses; defenses weakened by, of all things, a drug that promotes an erection.

Chapter IV: The Cult of the Beautiful Egg

I t is impossible to write about beauty without focusing upon what I call the cult of the beautiful egg. By way of background, let me say that the "egg" part of my terminology is uniquely biological and the "cult" part is uniquely sociological. The metaphor of the "beautiful egg" is a good one, because it does encompass both biology and sociology as it seeks to explain behavior of the sexes and everything that goes along with it, including beauty. The dynamics of the admixture of biology and sociology creates any number of psychological mechanisms which regulate our fascination with beauty.

To take the rich man/pretty woman match-up as just one example, this classic pairing between wealth and beauty is modulated and regulated by this cult. The cult of the beautiful egg, however, is not limited to those who are already beautiful or those men who have achieved wealth. In one sense, the rich man/pretty woman match-up equates with the "big" leagues; while on the other hand, less attractive women and their lower status and less wealthy targets and suitors, make up the minor leagues. The intensity with which some minor league games are played suggests something very powerful about the motivation to win, and informs us that wherever a person fits on the scales of beauty or wealth, intense emotions accompany the cult of the beautiful egg.

There is a timeless consistency to the cult of the beautiful egg. One can study how men and women mate, how women get along with one another, the customs of courtship or any other overview or specific segment of man's cultural history, and time and time again beauty is a dominant factor. For our purposes here we will focus on the beauty connection to the cult of the beautiful egg, because it provides not only a window, but a picture window, if you will, into mankind's fascination with beauty.

Mothers and daughters are inherently caught up in the cult of the beautiful egg. For example, a casual observer would find it remarkable that such a seemingly simple issue as when and how a daughter can put color on her lips could so often provide the backdrop for some of the worst emotional upsets between a mother and a daughter. It is the cult of the beautiful egg that fuels, with seemingly limitless energy, mother and daughter disputes over makeup, hemlines, necklines, shoes and any number of other modulators of beauty. Battles related to how daughters alter their beauty can and often do create rifts between mother and daughter that never completely heal. Almost by definition, virtually all significant battles between women are derivative of the cult of the beautiful egg.

The "cult" part of the cult of the beautiful egg finds its clearest example in the beauty business. Beauty pageants, the fashion industry, plastic surgery, makeup, wardrobe and everything else involved with beauty has a decisively competitive edge to it. Who are the competitors? The answer is: other eggs, and the men competing for those eggs. The "cult" part of the cult of the beautiful egg is a little more difficult to visualize than are other cults, because the cult of the beautiful egg is ubiquitous. This cult is everywhere, and since it is everywhere, it is hard to see where it is not. Most cults are isolated little cliques that can be easily distinguished from the culture at large. The assumptions of the isolated cult are often experienced as distinctly different than the assumptions of the dominant culture. However, when it comes to the cult of the beautiful egg, we are all living right in the middle of it, the biggest cult on the planet.

Anywhere you go, cosmetic beauty is synonymous with female sexual attractiveness, which is inextricably linked to reproduction. Understood this way, and keeping in mind the almost limitless reservoirs of energy allocated by Mother Nature for reproduction, it is no wonder that beauty resides at the center of the most important activity of life itself; that is, sustaining life.

The cult of the beautiful egg operates like a game, a very serious game, where the rules impose upon all the players. There are winners and losers, and the clock sometimes runs out. People cheat at this game, and the one thing about it that makes it very, very popular, is that it is fun. Long after the players can win the trophy, people still play the game because it is so much fun. Possessing beauty in the egg game is like being able to throw, catch, run, hit, and be coordinated, all at the same time.

"Egg," the word, can either be a noun or a verb. "Egging" is something that one egg does to another egg, and to other men. Egging begins surprisingly early. One's ability to be a good "egger" is directly linked to one's ability to be attractive. Ask any perceptive pre-school teacher and she will tell you how little girls have already begun practicing their craft before their fourth year of life. The art of egging is motivated in the first instance by biology, but is wholly defined by our culture. (SEE PHOTO OF CUTE KIDS)

Egg Wars

The ante is raised in the egging war every time the hem line is raised or the neckline plunges. The competition is fierce, ruthless, and unlike traditional war, no one is on your side. If the egg fashion war can be analogized to the Cold War of the latter part of the twentieth century, then what has occurred as we begin the twenty-first century is a heating up of the battle. For example, there was a time in America when only a certain kind of woman purchased risqué undergarments. As we embark upon the new millennium, however, the sexy lingerie business has become mainstream. The average woman, not the stripper, is the bread and butter customer of stores like Victoria's Secret. And it's not just Victoria's Secret—stores like Wal-Mart and Target routinely stock linge-

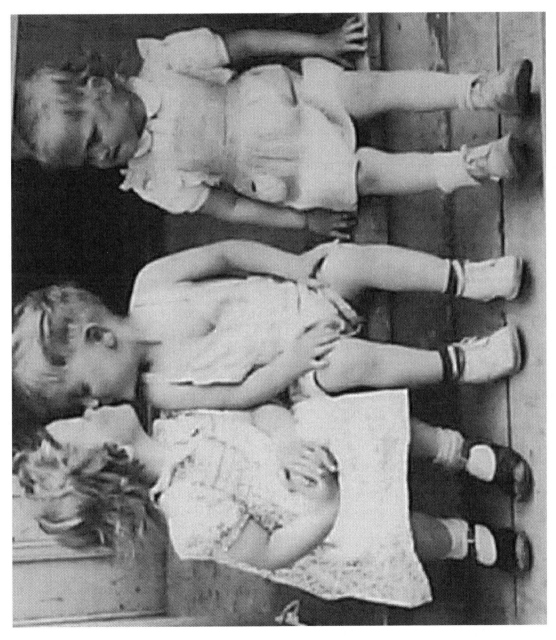

Egging Begins Very Early in Life

rie that just a few years ago could only be found at Frederick's of Hollywood.

According to L.A. Times Staff Writer Sarah Hale, as of the year 2000, 19 million North American women were wearing thong panties. Not too long ago, thongs were reserved for strippers or ladies of the evening. Not only are women wearing thongs in ever increasing numbers, but they are beginning to show them off. Hale noted that thong underwear has started to peek above pant lines on fashion runways and in urban nightclubs. Thongs represent the fastest-growing lingerie niche, according to Hale. Stores like Lane Bryant, a store that caters to bigger women, has gotten into the thong act. Lane Bryant sells thong panties in size 15. According to NPD Group Inc., a New York purchasing and research firm, sales of thong panties increased 156%, to 131 million dollars, between 1995 and 1999. Victoria's Secret reported that since 1995, their thong sales have risen 30%, while their more conservative panties have increased in sales only 5% over the same time frame.

The thong represents an "upping of the ante" in the battle to be sexy and alluring to men. Being sexy and alluring has become synonymous with being worthy. The competition has become so rampant that even pregnant women have entered the fray. According to Maternity Outfitters owner Lorraine Zistler, her store sells three pairs of thong panties for every one pair of regular underwear.

Freaking

America's teen girls are getting into the fray like never before. Perhaps one of the best examples of raising the egg-war ante is "freaking." For those readers who may not be familiar with this escalation of the egg wars, teen girls and their boyfriends engage in explicit coital movements on the dance floor. Freaking often includes touching and displays of underwear, including thong panties.

Across the United States, high school administrators are forced to grapple with this Defcon-2 escalation of the egg war. In an investigative article which appeared in the San Diego Union in the Spring of 2002, writer Eleanor Yang researched the "freaking" phenomenon. She interviewed dance historian Jonathan David Jackson. According to Jackson, the earliest forms of freaking were inspired by a movie named "Cooley High," along with the "House Party" movies. Jackson noted that freaking began in the late 1980's, but was limited to inner-city black schools. Freaking didn't create controversy until it reached white suburban schools in the 1990's.

I think it is important for the reader to distinguish this latest manifestation of the egg wars from earlier battle strategies and weapons during earlier generations. Freaking is not just another expression of teen sexuality, in the same way that doing the "twist" was, in its day, an expression of teen sexuality during the 1960's. Girls on American Bandstand who were engaged in the "egg dance" did not bend over, show their thong panties and a hint of pubic hair, in order to have a male thrust his pelvis against the exposed crotch of the teen girl bending over. But that is exactly one permutation of the latest upping of the egg war ante. Middle-class girls feel the pressure to compete in the arms race. A short skirt, even a mini-skirt, neither provides effective deterrent or threat by today's standards. By analogy, a mini-skirt is like a Gatling gun when confronted with the laser-guided missile-toting girl who is freaking on the dance floor. Janine Garafolo, the brilliant comedienne and social observer, commented after the airing of the 2002 MTV Music Awards broadcast that if women wear their pants any lower, they will be showing their vaginas. "Hello, see my vagina, hope you like me," observed Ms. Garafolo.

And where are boys in all of this? Boys have habituated on sexual expression because there is so much of it and it is so explicit. In study after study we have learned that boys and men "get used to" female expressions of sexuality. In the 1950's an occasional flash of skin, demarcated by the two inches above the knee, provided ample stimuli for fantasy and arousal for men and boys alike. Showing the thigh just won't "do it" for a teen girl in today's world, because boys simply don't respond. It takes more and more "stimuli" just to get noticed. As girls have become embroiled in the egg war, the all-out arms race has resulted in freaking, and as many parents are horrified to learn, actual combat.

The Center for Applied Behavioral and Evaluation Research, functioning as an outside contractor for The Centers for Disease Control in Atlanta Georgia, surveyed forty-six public schools in three cities in the Northeastern U.S. Data on psychosocial and behavioral outcomes collected from approximately 3,000 students at the beginning of seventh grade (baseline), at the end of seventh grade, and at the end of eighth grade. The data revealed that 38 percent of the boys and 14 percent of the girls had had sexual intercourse by the beginning of the seventh grade. (Source: The Center for Applied Behavioral and Evaluation Research, www.aed.org/).

Multiple studies show that the incidence of sexual intercourse among teens has continued to slow throughout the 1990s, leading parents and social observers to conclude that the egg war is really nothing more than a cold war. But sexual intercourse data do not tell the whole story about how the egg wars have heated up as we enter the new millennium. Data suggest that 25 percent of teen girls who report never having had sexual intercourse, have performed oral sex. Manual stimulation is so commonplace that it doesn't even show up on the researcher's radar screen, because like oral sex, it is not really considered sex at all. As the egg wars escalate, the soldiers become younger and younger and their behavior becomes more competitive.

Laura Session Stepp researched the incidence of oral sex in middle school. Writing for the Washington Post in an investigative article which appeared in the summer of 1999, Ms. Stepp interviewed Michael Schaeffer, a supervisor for health education in Prince George's County, Maryland, for the past 15 years. Schaeffer told Stepp that "It (referring to oral sex) is now the expected minimum behavior." Deborah Roffman, a human sexuality consultant to 15 schools in the Baltimore-Washington corridor, was also quoted by Stepp, "I've been teaching in schools for 30 years. I am receiving an increasing number of inquiries about incidents of oral sex among young adolescents, both at parties and occasionally at school." Patricia Hersch is the author of the book *A Tribe Apart: A Journey Into the Heart of American Adolescence.* She wrote that "To me, oral sex was more intimate than intercourse. Kids today absolutely don't see it that way. It's done commonly, with a shrug. It's part of the grab bag of sexual activities."

Teen Media

The proverbial chicken or egg question (no pun intended) begs to be asked when a review is made of magazines which target teens, especially teen girls. Such a review was made by Janet Saidi, a freelance writer, in the summer of 2002. Saidi studied the content of a number of magazines written for teen girls. What Ms. Saidi found illustrates that teen combatants in the egg wars have any number of reference works which coach them on becoming more competitive. Here is what Ms.Saidi found in her review: The June/July issue of *CosmoGirl* featured an article entitled "5 Kisses to Try." This article included a kiss called the "sugar addict," involving the transfer of candy from mouth to mouth. The "super steamer" kiss requires the mouth-to-mouth transfer of Frappucino and hot mocha drinks, preferably conducted in an out-of-the-way place in Starbucks. The "free faller" kiss encourages teen girls to make out in an elevator. The June 2002 cover girl on *Seventeen* Magazine, Kirsten Dunst, discusses her leading men and what it was like to kiss them. The British Magazine *J-17* included an article entitled: "I Got Off with a Boy in a Hanson T-shirt—Someone Just Kill Me Now Please." To quote Ms. Saidi: "Perhaps the only people who can actually benefit from these confessions are parents of teen girls. Here, they can read about their straight-A students sneaking out of the house, embarking on secret online relationships and avoiding arrest ("I lied to a cop" from an article in the teen magazine *Twist*)." One only need make a cursory review of the advertisers in teen magazines to understand that beauty or beauty-related products comprise the bulk of advertisers. How to be sexually attractive in both looks and behavior is the common theme which permeates popular teen magazines.

Writer Peter Moore studied none other than Radio Disney's air plays. Moore wrote about his 2002 assessment of content on Radio Disney with a preface which declared that he is NOT an uptight, cultural conservative; yet, he is forced to express concern about the content on a radio station that, after all, is Radio *Disney*. What Moore discovered is what we refer to as the escalation of the egg wars. One must conclude that the battle is raging when Radio Disney gets into the fray. By way of background, Radio Disney's target demographic includes six-to eleven-year-olds. Radio Disney has been known to use focus groups of children as young as six years old to test-market its music. Moore cited the lyrics of 14-year-old Aaron Carter, in the Radio Disney-aired "Not Too Young, Not Too Old." Carter raps: "I'm older now...come and show me body." Carter continues:

"Girl whatcha gonna do? Come and talk to me in the backseat-Baby Backstreet." Radio Disney gives artist Lil' Romeo lots of air play. Radio Disney airs the following lyrics from one of his songs: "Eleven years old, making A's and B's and these little mommies can't keep their hands off me. I'm a little boy but I live a big man's life...I got grown women wantin' to be in my life." According to Moore, Radio Disney edits selected portions of some of the more offensive lyrics, while continuing to play the bulk of the song, for example: the phrase "Am I sexual?" by the Backstreet Boys was edited, along with "You'll be kissing my..." by Pink. As of the writing of this book, Lil' Romeo's references to the backseat have been edited, while the song itself, which included the reference to the backseat, continues to be played on Radio Disney.

What is critical to understand here is that the sexualization of kids is inextricably linked to profit. To say it another way, there is money to be made when the egg war rages. Kids, especially girls, are steeped in a culture that demands that they be beautiful and alluring at all costs, no matter how far they have to go. An endless supply of products and advice is sold to teen girls, which will assure victory while at the same time encouraging that the battle continues to rage. As the egg war ante is continually raised, and as the warriors become younger and younger, American society is caught between its self-comforting belief that it protects and cherishes children—see, for example, the "Amber Alert" notification system—all the while promulgating a culture that makes children nothing more than sexualized cannon fodder to be harvested for profit.

The Hunter and Her Prey

Men are easy prey. The latter part of the twentieth century was punctuated with any number of powerful men who fell from power because of their involvement with a pretty woman. President Clinton, Bob Livingston, Gary Hart, Newt Gingrich, Jesse Jackson, Gary Condit and before him Wilbur Mills. All of these men succumbed to the alluring siren song of the egg, that is, the "beautiful" egg, wrapped in layer upon layer of makeup, hair, perfume, sexy clothing and a host of other cosmetic accruements that are designed to accomplish EXACTLY what was accomplished, attract and engage in mating behavior with a powerful man.

Why are we amazed, or even surprised for that matter, when a well-executed, well-honed and notoriously seductive plan achieves its goal? Why are we surprised that powerful and rich men succumb to beauty? After all, rich and powerful men ARE the target. Biology can be a very formidable opponent to even those who believe that succumbing to the allure of a beautiful woman is a sin...just ask Jim Baker or Jimmy Swaggert. Why are we amazed that those men who have been dealt out of the game by young sexy women are virtually always instrumental in exposing the failings of rich and powerful men at the hands of attractive seductresses? What is amazing is that the plan remains shrouded within a labyrinth of defenses. What is amazing is that sex and beauty are removed from the equation, and the whole matter is rendered into a conveniently rationalized discussion of poor character, violations of law or ethics.

At the root of all quests for beauty is the purpose of the egg to be desired, to be attractive, to be beautiful. Beauty and egg desirability are one and the same. The cult of the beautiful egg is uniquely able to harness all of the energy that one might imagine is allocated by Mother Nature to fuel the ultimate act of survival—reproduction. If the cult of the beautiful egg provides the ultimate answer as to why the emphasis is on beauty, the myriad of often subtle and remote egg behaviors which derive from the cult of the egg prove two things. It proves that the tentacles of the egg reach everywhere, and it shows that people have virtually no idea about the connection between what they do and why they do it.

As referenced earlier in this chapter, men have become numb to ever-escalating expressions of the egg wars. This process, which has a neurological basis, is termed "habituation." Presenting the same or ever-increasing sexual stimulus, over and over, creates a numbing to that stimulus. This is the reason for the counterintuitive finding that older men are generally easier to arouse when compared to younger men. Whereas an older man may find the hint of cleavage, the fluttering of eyes or the smell of enticing perfume to be arousing, the younger male, who has come of age in a society where he has been saturated with overt sexual images, may find the sight of the nipple, pubis or coital pose from a beautiful girl to be an insufficient stimulus for arousal. A casual walk along the beach boardwalk on a hot summer's day finds young men interacting with bikini-clad beauties as though they were his same-sex "buddies," while the older men are observed to be "rubber-necking" and tripping over people and obstacles alike because they can't keep their attention on anything else except the beautiful women. When it comes to the egg wars, men's habituation to ever-increasing expressions of sexuality proves the destructive nature of any unbridled arms race.

"War is hell," especially the egg war. Women, even if they prevail and defeat their adversaries, lose any number of important things in the bargain. They often lose their friends, and virtually always ruin the sense of sisterhood that can provide emotional sustenance. The egg war is made up of many unhappy warriors. The armies are full of women who don't really enjoy competing in an ever-escalating battle where necklines get lower and lower while breasts keep getting bigger and bigger, and where skirts predictably rise to reveal a scar in the form of a rose that was made in response to an ever-increasing need to remain competitive. Just like in conventional war, the arms race always ends in mutually assured destruction.

Chapter V: Plastic Surgery

Elective-aesthetic surgery is unique among all other types of surgery, because it is the only operation that is completely motivated by psychological desire. Because elective-aesthetic surgery is completely motivated by psychological factors, cosmetic surgery is unique among all of the medical specialties. It is important to distinguish requests for reconstructive plastic surgery on the one hand and elective-aesthetic plastic surgery on the other. The latter request for surgery is motivated purely by a desire to look differently. The former request is often motivated by a need for a cosmetic repair or to improve function. The two are not always mutually exclusive. For example, sometimes by cosmetically improving the nose the surgeon improves function. The same is true for some blepharoplasty (eye lid) and mastopexy (breast reduction) surgeries.

The motivation to have elective aesthetic surgery is the only surgery which is driven by a psychological dissatisfaction with one's looks. A psychological dissatisfaction is the driving force behind all elective-aesthetic surgeries. A person may feel bad because their nose is too big, their breasts are too small, their thighs are too fat, their eyes are too droopy, their chin recedes, their brow is furrowed, their cheekbones are ill-defined, their lips are too thin, or a virtually never-ending list of dissatisfactions with one's "look."

Feeling bad about one's looks may manifest in any number of ways. It may manifest as a feeling of insecurity in social situations. It may show up as depression, anxiety, shyness or limiting self-consciousness. It may manifest as an obsession with the area of the body which is the source of the dissatisfaction. Feeling bad may express itself as a stomach ache, a rash or any number of other physical symptoms, each of which is an expression of the patient's dissatisfaction with how they look. Feeling bad about one's body, if you are a woman, is epidemic in America. A majority of teenage girls, for example, believe and feel that they are fat and unattractive.

Cosmetic Surgery Statistics

The American Society for Aesthetic Plastic Surgery (ASAPS) compiles data on the surgical procedures performed by its members. According to the ASAPS, its members perform more cosmetic procedures than surgeons who belong to any other cosmetic/plastic surgery medical specialty board. The ASAPS is not, however, the only medical board whose members perform plastic and cosmetic surgery. With regard to board certification, the American Board of Medical Specializations, and the American Medical Association, certifies only one specialty board related to plastic and cosmetic surgery, named the American Board of Plastic Surgery (ABPS). The American

Society of Plastic Surgeons (ASPS), formed in 1931, states that it is the largest plastic surgery specialty organization in the world. The ASPS is only comprised of members certified by the American Board of Plastic Surgery, or an equivalent foreign board certification. The ASAPS, formed in 1967, states that its members are certified by the ABPS. The American Academy of Facial Plastic and Reconstructive Surgery (AAFPRS), states that it is the largest association of facial plastic and reconstructive surgeons, with more than 2,600 members, as of 2003. The AAFPRS is made up of members who specialize in cosmetic or plastic surgery, but who may or may not be certified by the ABPS. If the topic of board certification isn't confusing enough, consider that there exist scores of other specialty boards whose members perform cosmetic surgery.

The following data are presented here in order to provide the reader with a sense of not only the number of cosmetic procedures being performed in the United States, but also the types of surgery performed and the trends reflected in the cosmetic surgery data. Keep in mind that the total number of cosmetic procedures performed is higher than is reflected in the statistics quoted here.

According to the AAFPRS, men are responding to economic stress differently than are women. When comparing 2002 with 2001 data on men who chose to undergo cosmetic procedures, the organization's survey results found a 497 percent increase in fat injections to eliminate frowns, an 88 percent increase in Botox injections to smooth wrinkles, a 79 percent increase in microdermabrasion and 13 percent increase in laser resurfacing of skin. Men were more than twice as likely as women to report that the reason for choosing facial cosmetic surgery was for work-related reasons. The AAFPRS also reported a trend where husband and wife couples, and mother and daughter pairs, chose to undergo cosmetic surgery together. Thirty-one percent of AAFPRS members reported that they had seen patients who received cosmetic surgery as a present.

According to the ASAPS, nearly 6.9 million sugical and non-surgical procedures were performed in 2002, with a 22.8 percent increase from 1997 to 2002. The top five cosmetic surgical procedures were as follows: Liposuction: 372,831, up 11 percent since 1997; Breast Augmentation: 249,641, up 147 percent since 1997; Eyelid Surgery: 229,092, up 44 percent since 1997; Rhinoplasty Surgery (nose job): 156,973, up 15 percent since 1997; and Breast Reduction Surgery: 125,614, up 162 percent since 1997.

The top five non-surgical cosmetic procedures performed in 2002 by ASAPS physicians were as follows: Botox injections: 1,658,667, up 2446 percent since 1997; Microdermabrasion: 1,032,417, up 13 percent since 1997; Collagen Injections, 793,120; Laser Hair Removal, 736,458; and Chemical Peel, 495,415.

With regard to gender, women underwent 88 percent of all the surgery performed by ASAPS members, for a total of 6.1 million cosmetic procedures in 2002. Men had 12 percent of the total number of cosmetic surgeries performed by ASAPS members, which totaled 800,000.

Further demographic analysis showed that "baby boomers" (ages 35-50) had the most procedures, with 44 percent of the total. Men and women age 51-64 had 25 percent of procedures. People between the ages of 19 and 34 had 22 percent of the cosmetic procedures. Those over the age of 65 had about 5 percent of the procedures performed; and those age 18 and under accounted for 3.5 percent of the total number of cosmetic procesures.(SEE ASAPS GRAPHS)

People of color accounted for 17 percent of all cosmetic procedures, broken down as follows: Hispanics, 7 percent; African-Americans, 5 percent; Asians, 4 percent; and other non-Caucasians, at 1 percent.

Non-Medical Complications from Plastic Surgery

When most people think of complications from plastic surgery, they think of things like visible scars, asymmetrical breasts or infections. There is another type of complication, however, that can be just as painful as a medical complication. Psychological complications are often subtle and counterintuitive.

Psychological problems, the result of a poor surgical result, make intuitive sense, given what we know about the relationship between beauty and how we feel about ourselves. However, what dynamics are at work when the surgical result is near perfect, and still a psychological complication results? The following case studies illustrate the fascinating effects beauty can have on our lives.

Loss of Cultural Identity

One such perfect result occurred when a rhinoplasty was performed on a Middle-Eastern woman who requested that her anterograde nasal bridge and matching nasal tip be shaped into a petite and sculpted nose, typical of a Barbie doll. The surgeon performed the operation and achieved a brilliant result. The nose was beautiful in proportion and fit well with her overall facial structure. The patient loved her nose, at least at first. Shortly after the surgery, however, the patient developed a number of psychological problems, including depression and anxiety. What went wrong?

Unwittingly, this patient not only had her nose reshaped, but she also had her cultural identity reshaped in the process. As a member of a large family with close cultural ties to her Middle-Eastern heritage, the new nose became a symbol of an alien culture. This patient's inherited nose was tantamount to membership in the family. Once the nose changed, family members saw the patient differently. She was no longer "one of us." Without her familial nose, the family began to experience a kind of plastic surgery created xenophobia, directed at their operated-on family member. The patient and the family thought the nose was attractive; some even acknowledged that it was more attractive than the patients' God-given nose. However, everyone agreed that it was not a "Middle-Eastern" nose. What is important in this case is that the patient had not consciously rejected her Middle-Eastern cultural membership when she chose her new nose. Moreover, none of

American Society for Aesthetic Plastic Surgery
Cosmetic Surgery Data

COSMETIC SURGERY TRENDS

Number of Procedures

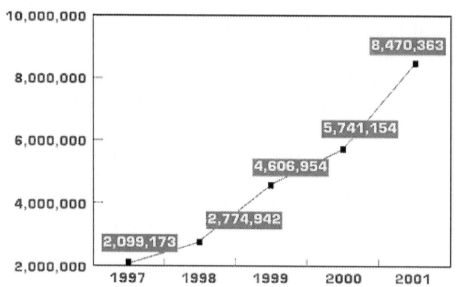

Source: American Society for Aesthetic Plastic Surgery

TOP 5 COSMETIC SURGICAL PROCEDURES IN 2001

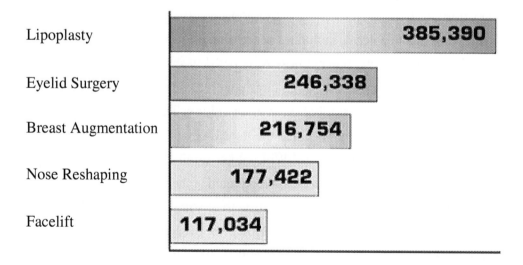

Lipoplasty — 385,390
Eyelid Surgery — 246,338
Breast Augmentation — 216,754
Nose Reshaping — 177,422
Facelift — 117,034

her family had a *conscious* chauvinistic allegiance to their particular cultural and genetic beauty. Once this patient had surgery, however, it became clear to everyone that the nose was a powerful symbol of membership in the family, and her "new" nose wasn't a valid membership card. Without her membership card she was ostracized from her family. A date with a non Middle-Easterner became just one more example of her mythical rejection of her family, whereas before the surgery, no one in her family gave significance to her cross-cultural dating. Even here, however, Western culture is making inroads, and the experience of this patient may soon become a thing of the past.

Elaine Sciolino, a writer for the New York Times, has reported on the incidence of elective-aesthetic plastic surgery in the most unlikely of places and cultures, conservative Iran. Women living in Iran are required, by law, to cover their hair and to wrap their body in loose clothing (Chador), in order to conceal their womanly shape. The nose, however, remains visible. Even considering religious and cultural edicts to the contrary, the "nose job" has become all the rage among Iranian women as we enter the early part of the twenty-first century. Sciolino writes: "Rhinoplasty, in particular, has become so widespread that the Iranian feminist magazine *Zanan* devoted an eight-page article to the subject in its August 2000 issue. The cover showed an artificial nose superimposed on the face of a woman. The headline read, 'Young Women and Men and the Hot Market in Nose Jobs.'" And what kind of nose do the surgeons attempt to create? The answer: the petite, retrograde and sculpted nose typical of the Western *model du jour.*

It is not just plastic surgery that has infiltrated conservative Iranian culture. Hot selling books on beauty, such as "Face-Lifts Without Surgery" and "The Secrets of Being Young and Beautiful," are all the rage in Iran. Sciolino's investigation found that even if Iranian women do not resort to plastic surgery, they often invest heavily in hair dressers, aerobics classes, makeup, clothes and lingerie. Colored contact lenses, made in America and available without a prescription at Iranian pharmacies for about $15 a pair, are best sellers for both women and men. One Iranian woman named Lili, referenced in Sciolino's research, was quoted as saying: "I want a smaller nose, like a doll's nose. I'm willing to pay lots of money to a plastic surgeon to give me a new look. I don't want to have any faults in my face. I'd like to look beautiful, like Marilyn Monroe."

Gender Identity

Gender issues are often intertwined with the request for plastic surgery. Take for example the young man who showed up for a consultation desirous of a second operation to his abdomen. He felt that too much fat had been taken out of his abdomen in a prior lipoplasty surgery performed by another surgeon. Looking at this patient, the objective observer only saw a flat and "ripped" abdomen. The patient reported that after his first surgery he felt "different and no longer himself." The patient begged to have fat put back into his abdominal area. Since the surgery to remove fat from his abdomen he had developed a severe depression, contemplated suicide and had thought about little else except restoring his abdomen to its prior condition. What was going on?

This patient had a long-standing ambivalence about his gender identity. He vacillated back and forth between his identification with being a male or female. During one of his male identification periods he had decided to have the surgery to make his abdomen more male. This patient's abdomen was the area where the psychological battle between the sexes took place. The surgery worked; it worked so well that the female part of the battle had been defeated. This patient possessed a feminine side that was traditional, and a throwback to the days when women were more shapely and curvaceous. When the surgeon aspirated abdominal fat, he not only removed fat, but he had also removed this person's feminine personality.

The old saw about never appreciating what you have until you lose it, never applied more. Once this psychological complication was identified, a medical question had to be answered: Where would the fat come from to replace the lost fat in his abdomen? The patient showed anxiety when the derriere was suggested as a place from which to harvest fat. That area, though not the primary area of his feminine identity, was still a gender-balanced part of his body. After much thought, the thighs were chosen as the area from which to harvest fat. Why? It seems that no American woman, not even our patient's feminine side, likes fat thighs. The fat was removed from the thighs, applied evenly over the abdominal area and voila, within a few weeks, the patient was off anti-depressants, had returned to an active life and had begun the battle again with his masculine side.

Marriage

Changing one's body can affect not only the patient, but everyone around her as well. Enter the dentist's wife and her husband for a breast augmentation surgery. After 20 years of marriage, the wife had become dissatisfied with her breasts. The missus appeared with little makeup and a conservative hairdo. She wore a muted beige pants outfit with matronly shoes and tan hose. Her nails were not painted, and they were short. Her husband did not share her dissatisfaction with her breasts but was willing to go along with her desire for surgical enhancement if "that would make her happy." Boy, did it make her happy.

The surgery was completed, and within six weeks after the surgery the dentist appeared at our office complaining that his wife was having an affair with her guitar teacher. He reported that she no longer attended church with the family, and that she had stopped preparing dinner. The wife showed up for a two month follow-up, and the metamorphosis in personality was shocking.

The conservative dentist's wife had blossomed into a casting director's dream come true for a middle-aged stripper. She showed up in a red micro-mini dress that was low cut and clinging. She squirmed out of her dress before her examination gown could be given to her and before her surgeon and I could leave the examining room, as was our prescribed practice. Underneath the dress was a lingerie collection right out of Frederick's of Hollywood, complete with black garter belts. The surgical result was very nice. Over the next several months, several new breast augmentation patients were referred by this woman who, by this time, had left her husband. Evidently, this patient made a habit of going around showing her new breasts to anyone and everyone, and passing out the surgeon's name who performed the surgery. Her life had changed, and so had her husband's. The children lost their conservative mother and the dentist lost his wife. The guitar teacher got a girlfriend, at least for a time, and the surgery practice got several new breast enhancement patients.

Sometimes less than optimal surgical results can create a very happy patient. Dr. William Morain, a gifted plastic surgeon and past editor of the Annals of Plastic Surgery, has written that one of his most satisfied patients had nipples pointing in different directions. One nipple pointed to Calgary, and the other to Key West. Dr. Morain reported that this patient was so happy that she showed her breasts to everyone, thus diverting any number of would-be patients from his practice. Dr. Morain's anecdotal story, along with my own research, shows that satisfaction with one's plastic surgery is an internal process, not necessarily directly related to the objective result. Surgeons are often flabbergasted to have achieved an exquisite surgical result, only to have a dissatisfied patient, but this is what occurs with an ever-increasing frequency in today's plastic surgery environment.

If elective plastic surgery seems dominated more by feelings and emotions than by physical medicine, it is. The change which comes from plastic surgery occurs inside, not on the outside. When cosmetic surgery has a profound effect, it achieves that effect by changing self-concept. The surgeon may have operated on the nose, but it was the mind that he changed. Two cup sizes bigger may mean womanhood for the patient. Thinner thighs may mean lovable rather than rejectable. Enhanced lips mean "I am kissable." It also means, to the informed observer, that the patient may have felt unkissable at one time, and concluded that the best way to make themselves kissable was to alter a visual cue rather than all of the other things that could have been changed. The request for lip surgery almost always involves the request to make them bigger. Actually, to be more precise, the request is to make the lips "purse," as if the lips were in a kissing pose. This is accomplished by "puffing up" the lips with the insertion of muscle tissue, autologous fat injections or various other substances.

With reference to lip and breast enhancement patients, I reflect upon the work of Tinbergen, an ethologist who studied a little fish named the Stickleback. In one of Tinbergen's famous experiments, he made a plastic replica of the female Stickleback fish, with one difference. In the plastic fish, Tinbergen made the abdomen much bigger. A big abdomen, it seems, acts as a sexual cue to the male Stickleback fish. Tinbergen put the plastic fish with the exaggerated abdomen in a tank with living female Sticklebacks which had beautiful, but normally sized abdomens. Tinbergen found that the male Sticklebacks were more attracted to the plastic fish, even though she wasn't real, couldn't reproduce and didn't respond, like the real fish, to the male fish's sexual overtures.

The natural Stickleback fish must have been perplexed over the inattention paid to her just because a plastic fish with a "voluptuous" abdomen had been put in the tank. Lips and breasts are imbued by men and women alike, in America and much of the world, with sexual meaning.

Surgically enhancing lips, breasts and even making a derriere protrude, may work for the same reason that Tinbergen's plastic fish captured the attention of the male suitor. So, do women with enhanced lips kiss more? Actually, they kiss less often. For one thing, these women seem protective of their lips. They don't want anything to interfere with the particular form and contour, not to mention the coloring that is typically applied in great abundance on operated-on lips. Also, the personality of women who have their lips enhanced is characteristically coquettish, dramatic and standoffish. Such is just one of the many ironies found in the beauty business. If male Stickleback fish could talk, they may report a similar experience as do men who become intimate with women who have enhanced their lips and breasts.

Parents and Their Children

Sometimes patients have absolutely no desire to change those things that could be improved. One day a young boy came in for a quick stitch-up for a playground accident when the surgeon noticed that his ears protruded almost perpendicular from his head. The surgeon, understanding how cruel some children can be, offered to perform an otoplasty on the boy's ears. Knowing that the little boy came from a poor family, the surgeon offered his services for virtually free, out of the goodness of his heart. The next day, the surgeon's nurse rushed into his office and informed him that an irate man was in the waiting room demanding to see him. The surgeon went out to find a man standing in his waiting room with ears perpendicular to his head. The first words out of his mouth were: "What is wrong with my boy's ears?"

The Mother with the Buxom Daughter

One day a mother and daughter appeared for a surgery consultation. The mother had urged her daughter to consult a plastic surgeon about having a mastopexy, or breast reduction surgery. There were three things about this consultation that jumped out at me. First, the desire to have surgery was exclusively the desire of the mother. Secondly, the daughter's breasts, though large, were perfectly formed and beautifully healthy. Finally, the daughter was only 15 years old. The mother did virtually all the talking in the consultation. Her arguments in favor of her daughter's surgery involved her observation that obviously her daughter's figure, most notably her breasts, made her very attractive to boys.

Mother had noticed that boys had looked at her daughter in a "sexual" way. When the daughter was asked to disrobe, the mother pointed out that her daughter's breasts resembled the breasts one would see in Playboy magazine. The daughter remained silent throughout the consultation, until she was asked by myself if she thought her breasts needed to be operated on. I had no sooner asked that question when the mother interrupted and asked, rather pointedly: "What do you mean, *operated* on?" I told her that making the kind of changes she was talking about would require an operation, of course. The mother replied: "Yes, but you don't need to say it that way." I asked about father's opinion about all of this. The mother didn't hesitate in telling me that her daughter has her father wrapped around her little finger, and that if she didn't want this then he would support her decision. I will note for the record that not only were the daughter's breasts large and beautifully formed, but her daughter was physically attractive, as well. Neither of these descriptions fit the mother. She was small-breasted and unattractive.

Seldom do we see such a blatant example of a mother's jealously of her daughter's beauty. Breasts are icons in the beauty business. They are conveniently symbolic of beauty and the desire that it generates in men. This is what the mother was reacting to, the fact that others found her daughter to be attractive and therefore gave her attention. Mother was jealous and had decided to level the playing field by attacking one symbolic source of her daughter's beauty. The daughter had no idea that she was even on the same playing field as her mother. Little did she know that when it comes to beauty, every woman is on the same playing field. Mother-daughter, friend-friend, teacher-student, doctor-patient, or virtually any other relationship you can think of.

When is Enough, Enough?

Some patients are plastic surgery junkies. No sooner have they completed one procedure than do they begin the anticipation of the next. Often these individuals begin their career as professional patient: already beautiful, but not beautiful enough. Something is lacking. The patient knows it, others see it, but no one knows exactly what it is. Surgeons seldom see it or find it salient to their practice. After all, surgeons are exactly that: surgeons. For the most part they see flesh and bone, and it is flesh and bone that they change. Plastic surgeons often have little appreciation of the fact that this type of professional plastic surgery consumer has come looking for her missing part at the operating theater. She has learned that her inner world is inextricably linked to her beauty. She feels better when she exercises vigorously, when she gets a tan, when she is primping in front of the mirror and when people look at her adoringly. It is only logical that the plastic surgeon possesses the magic formula for happiness. And request it she does, time and time again.

Give and Take

Plastic surgery is full of psychological nuance. The simple distinction of either adding or removing body tissue carries with it profound psychological meaning. For example, thigh (lateral femorals) and hip (iliac crests) reduction surgeries are two of the most commonly requested procedures in plastic surgery. Reducing the size of an area of the body does not have the same psychological significance as does augmenting an area of the body. When a patient asks that an area of the body be reduced in size, she is asking that a negative be removed. When a patient asks for an augmentation of a body area, she is asking for the addition of a positive. In other words, a patient who asks for bigger breasts is asking for the addition of something that she will carry with her. When that same patient asks for thinner thighs, she is asking that a problem be removed or taken away forever. The augmentation patient wants to show something off, the patient who asks for a reduction wants something to be hidden. The augmentation patient doesn't want to forget, but that is exactly what the reduction patient wants to do.

Reconstructive plastic surgery patients often obsess upon their deformity until a successful plastic surgery. After the repair, the obsession stops and the patient moves on. The augmentation patient may also obsess about a body part, but after a successful surgery the patient continues to obsess on their new addition. Rather than moving on, the patient becomes addicted to the new body part. That patient will nurture and focus upon her "new" body part. She will monitor and be exquisitely sensitive to the aging process, thus assuring that she will protect her investment with subsequent maintenance surgeries.

Scars

Scars have an importance above and beyond their physical size and shape. Scars possess various medical and psychological properties. Scars are defined, in part, by the following properties: 1. Contour. This includes direction, length, width and overall shape. 2. Contrast Color. This includes the relative color contrast of the scar within the context of surrounding tissue, e.g., hypo (light) or hyper (dark) pigmentation. 3. Topography. This involves the three-dimensional property of the scar, e.g., raised or indented, rough or smooth. 4. Contextual Placement. This term refers to where on the human body the scar exists.

Scars are also defined by the following psychological properties: 1. The patient's cognitive and emotional link to the source of the scar. This factor takes into consideration the affective circumstances surrounding the acquisition of the scar. If the scar was obtained during a fearful or uncontrollable event in the person's life, the scar naturally becomes associated with those original emotions and thoughts. The mere sight of the scar is enough to elicit the original emotions experienced during the acquisition of the scar. 2. Society's cognitive and emotional link to the source of the scar. This factor takes into consideration society's value judgment related to the affective circumstances surrounding the acquisition of the scar. If the scar was obtained during a socially disapproved or frowned upon event, the scar naturally becomes associated with those original emotions and thoughts. For example, if a robber obtains a scar on his face, suffered when his victim scratched him, then the scar becomes a living reminder of the original illegal act itself, despite the fact that the perpetrator may have rehabilitated himself. The converse is also true. For example, a Medal of

Honor winner who obtained a scar while carrying out an act of heroism may feel very good about his scar and not wish to improve its appearance. 3. The scar's impact upon the social and/or personal desirability of the patient. Scars routinely affect attractiveness. If the scar makes the person feel less attractive, then the scar has a direct effect upon self-esteem, confidence and social affiliation. This effect is intensified when the scar is located on highly valenced areas of the body, especially those areas that provide primary and secondary sexual cues.

Scars impact beauty in ways that are significantly different than a mere imperfection at the hands of mother nature. When a troublesome scar is significantly improved the patient feels as though a weight has been removed from her shoulders. When patients are informed that their problematic scar cannot be improved, they often experience depression and a loss of self-esteem, among other psychological symptoms. This is particularly true if the scar is located on a highly valenced part of the human body.

Plastic Surgery Advertisements

Advertisements for plastic surgery often incorporate classic marketing strategies. Cosmetic surgery ads comprise a repository of examples of how insecurity about beauty can be used to sell almost anything, including surgery. Our purpose here is to not provide an exhaustive exposé on the psychology of advertising. Rather, our focus is on the relationship between selling surgery and our feelings about beauty. One of the more interesting facts about the enclosed collage of advertisements is that they all appeared in the same Southern California newspaper over a two-month period of time. Cursory reviews of some of the more classic advertising strategies are helpful, because these classic gambits used in selling have not fallen on deaf ears when it comes to physician clients.

Some surgeons offer "specials." A special is designed to entice the consumer into buying a product or service because, in part, the offer is too good to pass up. Two-for-one ads represent a classic example of the special offer. Seasonal opportunity, as a marketing enticement, encompasses Christmas sales, Memorial Day "Blowouts," etc. The special occasion is promoted as a reason to offer a special price or bonus gift. Sometimes seasonal and special offer ads are combined in hybrid form. For example, "Two for the price of one" is the advertising copy for a Mother's Day special which incorporated both the special offer and seasonal opportunity gambits. This ad offered either mom or "someone" (including yourself) a gift certificate for two of a series of cosmetic enhancement procedures. (SEE PHOTO CREDIT OF PLASTIC SURGERY GIFT CERTIFICATE ADVERTISEMENT AND SPECIAL SPRING PRICING AD)

Exclusivity is yet another advertising gambit. Here, the potential consumer is enticed with the promise of getting the best, something unique, something exceptional. "Transforming art into reality" implies an ideal outcome. One ad touted "Exceptional Surgery...Exceptional Results." "Excellence in Plastic Surgery" simply states the promise. (SEE PHOTO CREDIT OF "TRANS-

FORMING ART INTO REALITY" AND "EXCEPTIONAL" PLASTIC SURGERY ADVER-TISEMENTS) One gambit shared by cosmetic and laser eye surgeons, along with some dentists, is the "easy" gambit. Here the surgeon promises an operation that is not only convenient but quick and uninvolved. "48-HOUR FACE-LIFT" is the banner for an ad which touted a "quick recovery; excellent for younger patients; no loss of work (back in 2-3 days) and done without hospital or anesthesia fees." (SEE PHOTO CREDIT OF "48 HOUR" PLASTIC SURGERY ADVERTISE-MENT) I draw the reader's attention to the copy which references hospital and anesthesia fees. To those of us who know, what this means is that this surgeon most likely does his surgery in his office or surgical center, and may not utilize an M.D. anesthesiologist in his practice. Moreover, one wonders if the "quick recovery" is something that only "younger patients" can expect, not those who may be older.

In addition to classic advertising strategies, like those listed above, the marketing of cosmetic surgery preys upon its potential client's insecurities about their own beauty. This approach is widespread and taps into self-consciousness and insecurity about personal beauty. Many ads incorporate beautiful models. Often, these ads incorporate advertising copy which taps into fears about how others will perceive your body. "Shape up for Summer!" is just one example of utilizing the gentle reminder that summer is associated with more body exposure and thus, more of an opportunity to be self-conscious about one's looks.

"Ready for the Beach?" is another example of this tact. (SEE "SHAPE UP FOR SUM-MER" AND "READY FOR THE BEACH" PLASTIC SURGERY ADVERTISEMENTS) Some cosmetic surgery ads simply come out and state the fear underlying some patient's motivation to have surgery, for example: "Sculpt Away Ugly Fat From Your Stomach, Hips and Thighs!" (SEE "SCULPT AWAY UGLY FAT" PLASTIC SURGERY ADVERTISEMENT) Some ads simply promise what every woman wants: beauty. "Be beautiful with Botox" reads one ad…what could be more simple and to the point? (SEE PHOTO CREDIT OF BOTOX PLASTIC SURGERY AD-VERTISEMENT)

Other advertisements have sought to incorporate my research into their advertising copy. One ad used a photo of a woman with the caption: "I didn't want to look different, just better." This ad came from my research, which demonstrated that when a patient wants the surgeon to make her into a different "kind" of person, that request is frequently the harbinger of any number of problems which make these patients poor candidates for cosmetic surgery. (SEE PHOTO CREDIT OF "I DIDN'T WANT TO LOOK DIFFERENT" PLASTIC SURGERY ADVERTISEMENT) Another ad, previously referenced herein, sought to incorporate my work which investigated the desire of an ever-growing number of patients to have cosmetic surgery that is often termed "over the top" surgery because of its "operated on" look. (SEE PHOTO CREDIT OF "EXCEPTIONAL SURGERY" PLASTIC SURGERY ADVERTISEMENT) The very talented surgeon who utilized

Plastic Surgery Advertisements

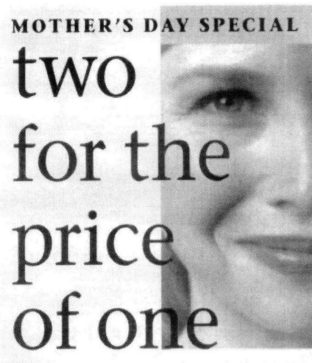

MOTHER'S DAY SPECIAL

two for the price of one

Give your mom or another special "someone" (including yourself) a gift certificate for a Botox®, Microdermabrasion, Photofacial™ Skin Rejuvenation, Spider Vein Removal or Hair Reduction Treatment and receive the second treatment absolutely **FREE!**

Botox® —For lines and wrinkles

Microdermabrasion
~Reveals new, younger-looking skin

Photofacial™ Skin Rejuvenation
~Reduces signs of aging and sun damage

Spider Vein Removal
~Noninvasive and effective

Unwanted Hair Reduction
~Long-lasting and gentle

Call to learn about our upcoming Botox® parties!

Now you can have beautiful skin at the speed of light!

Ready For The Beach?

Plastic Surgery Advertisements

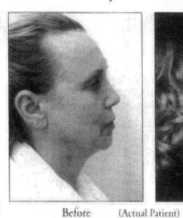 

Plastic Surgery Advertisements

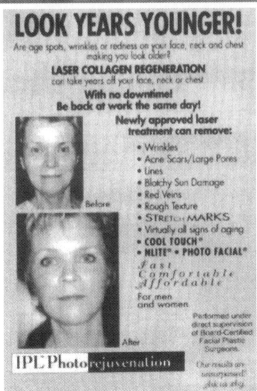

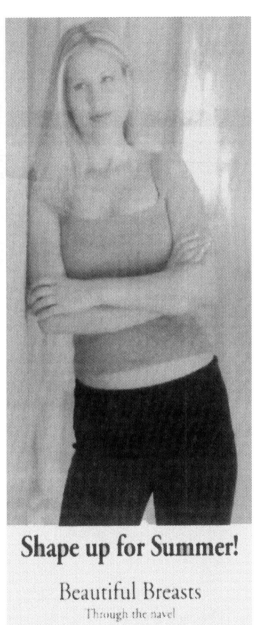

Plastic Surgery Advertisements

I Didn't Want To Look Different, Just Better!

This Advertisement Incorporates Findings From My Research.
It Suggests that Looking Better is a Much Preferred Motivation to Have Cosmetic Surgery
Than is the Desire to Look Different

Plastic Surgery Advertisements

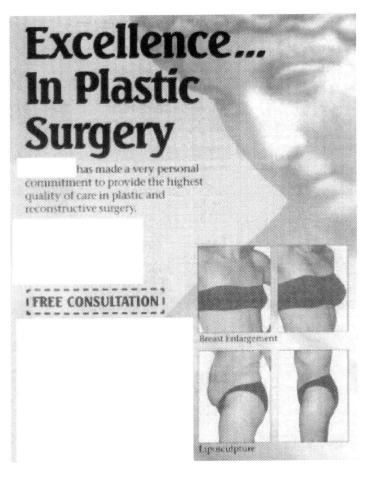

This "Excellence" Ad Suggests an Exclusive Experience Awaits

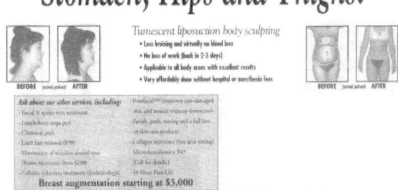

This *Ugly* Ad Strips Away any Pretense

Plastic Surgery Advertisements

Exceptional Surgery
Exceptional Results

"Cosmetic surgery results should look both natural and dramatic."

If you are considering cosmetic surgery, you should expect results that are both natural and dramatic. It should not look "surgical" or "done". You should be able to see examples of the surgeon's work that truly inspire confidence and trust.

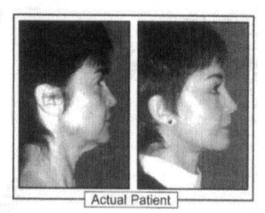

Actual Patient

This Advertisement Suggests that the Patient May Achieve a Dramatic Look Without Looking "Operated On." It May Also Unrealistically Raise Patient Expectations.

the ad, which touted the notion that surgery can be BOTH dramatic and natural, had been a supervising surgeon of a resident who performed a meloplasty (forehead lift). The supervising surgeon, noting the resident's "operated on" result, was reminded by the resident that today's patients want their work "over the top." Yet another advertisement which sought to elicit a more positive motivation to have surgery relied upon my research with older patients. I had noted in that research that one of the more healthy reasons to undego elective plastic surgery, not only for older people, but in general,was to look as good as you feel.

Just as some of my research findings have been incorporated into cosmetic surgery ads, some of my research findings have been ignored. For example, my work has shown that a patient's ultimate satisfaction with their plastic surgery is a function of their expectations. Specifically, realistic expectations predict satisfied patients, while unrealistic expectations predict the greater likelihood of patient dissatisfaction.

Anything that a surgeon does to unrealistically inflate his patient's expectations may be good for getting new patients, but may well prove to cause post-operative problems when it comes to patient satisfaction. Thus, one can see that exclusivity advertising may prove to be problematic in the long run. This type of advertising draws into a medical practice people who have a tendency toward unrealistic expectations. Given the fact that not every result can be exceptional, and that complications do occur, the surgeon may be setting himself up for patients who may be less than satisfied, even when the result is very good. I developed a test to assess patient expectations named the Napoleon Preoperative Test, or NPT. That test asks patients to draw themselves as they would realistically look after surgery, and as they would ideally look after surgery. The test is useful in any number of ways, but perhaps most importantly, it often exposes the patient who has unrealistic expectations about the outcome of their surgery. This can be seen, for example, when patients ignore the difference between a realistic and an ideal outcome by simply equating the two on the test. (SEE PHOTO CREDIT OF THE NAPOLEON PREOPERATIVE TEST)

Every nuance which is part and parcel of the complex and often counterintuitive world of beauty enters into the world of the plastic surgeon. Surgeons are ill-equipped to handle these difficult and troubling patient dynamics. But regardless of the surgeon's ability to handle the richly complex psychological world of their patients, those same patients project upon the surgeon their wants, wishes, desires, needs, fears, rationalizations and defense mechanisms. As I have written elsewhere, "On any given day, a surgeon may find himself cast as a parent, a lover, a competitor, or an authority figure to be conquered. And lest we forget, plastic surgeons are engaged in a seamless feedback loop with their potential patients when it comes to defining the beautiful image. Not only do surgeons help to create the public's conception of the ideal image through their work and in their advertisements, but sometimes they simply come out and give it a name. In 2001, The American Academy of Facial Plastic and Reconstructive Surgery named Catherine Zeta-Jones (See our

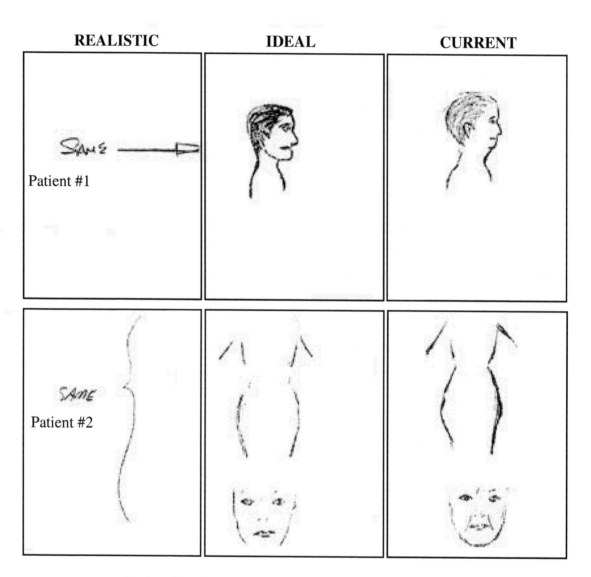

Patient Drawings from the Napoleon Preoperative Test

chapter on *Aging*) "the ideal face of femininity." The academy cited Zones' "short delicate jaw with small chin and nose, plus her lavish lips, well-developed cheek bones and prominent eyes."

Chapter VI: Aging

Beauty, youth and economics are logical bed-fellows. Youth and beauty are made synonymous by virtue of the impact that joining the two has on economics. With each tick of the clock, a new product is developed which promises to turn back the clock. Aging and our hatred of the effect it has on beauty is the greatest economic boon to the beauty industry since the development of the photograph. Aging is bad because of the effect it has on beauty and health, in that order.

When do people begin to get old? Once again, culture helps to define what most of us term old. Despite being qualified for a senior discount or social security, if you look beautiful your chronological age doesn't matter. There remains only one surefire way to avoid the stigma of aging—don't look your age. Consider for a moment that in the absence of visual cues which betray our chronological age, the entire concept becomes academic for those looking at us. Look young and act young, and you are young.

During my research on the subject of elderly cosmetic surgery patients, I noted some of the subtle ways our culture defines aging. First of all, it is firmly established that the label of "elderly" is associated with many negative stereotypes in the United States. It seems that older persons themselves subscribe to these negative stereotypes, to an even greater degree than do younger persons. Income seems to affect the perception of age. Some researchers have found that working class Americans identified old age as starting at age 60, while higher socioeconomic status groups estimate old age as starting at 70 years of age.

One of the tried and true aphorisms about aging is that "you are as young as you feel." Well, not exactly. After all, if you feel good but look like a casting agent's ideal for an "old man," you will be treated like an "old man." Satchel Paige was quoted as saying that "age is mind over matter; if you don't mind, it don't matter." That is easier said than done when the treatment you receive from others is, to a large degree, defined by how you look.

Not only do others define their treatment of you based upon your attractiveness, but how you look to yourself helps to define how you feel about yourself. The "looking glass self" is a hundred-year-old model in human behavior which describes, in part, how self-concept develops. The idea is that the treatment we receive from others is used as information that forms the basis for our beliefs about ourselves. For example, if people are constantly asking if you feel OK, then you begin to develop a self-concept that you don't look healthy and, therefore, may not be healthy.

In 1990, I wrote a paper which looked closely at the elderly cosmetic surgery patient. At that time I asserted that there were two general categories of cosmetic surgery patients. The first patient group is recognized by their effective overall social functioning, and reports having a subjective age set that is younger than their chronological years. I wrote that patients in this group may report that they feel like they are 40 years of age, even though they are in fact much older. The second group of patients presents a social background that appears to be no longer functional, and is isolated to varying degrees. This patient may report that sometimes they feel older than their chronological age. I concluded that this last group of patients may expect that by merely changing their appearance, they will regain a more positive internal state. Clearly, from the surgeon's perspective, the "safest" older patient to operate on is the one who wants to look as good as she feels.

The loss of beauty due to age means that you are excluded from many potential social roles. You are no longer as likely to be thought of as a wife, a girlfriend or desired sexual mate. You are found to be peculiar or odd if you engage in activities reserved for the young and beautiful. Rollerblading on the beach boardwalk is noticed as peculiar, as is wearing a provocative dress. The fact of the matter is that in highly image conscious geographical areas, such as Southern California and the large metropolitan areas of the Northeast, for example, an older person who looks her age may in fact feel miserable, almost exclusively because of how our youth-obsessed society bombards the older person with a never-ending barrage of toxic messages and images. When you begin to lose your beauty due to aging, others begin to treat you differently. The person who has lost her beauty due to age becomes a type of person as opposed to an individual. You are no longer known by your name, but thought of by your label, for instance, "old timer."

There exist huge gender differences when it comes to aging and loss of beauty. No profession feels this difference more acutely than do actresses and models. Pairing 65-year-old men with 25-year-old actresses in a love affair relationship is commonplace in Hollywood. Sean Connery, a man in his seventies as of the writing of this book, was consistently rated as one of the sexiest men in Hollywood in both his sixth and seventh decades of life. In 1999, he co-starred with Catherine Zeta-Jones in the movie *Entrapment.* In that movie, Connery and Jones, who is approximately 40 years younger than Connery, fall in love with one another. (SEE PHOTO CREDIT OF SEAN CONNERY AND CATHERINE ZETA-JONES) Jane Fonda, when she was in her fifties, was admired for "how well she looked for her age." That is as good as it gets for women.

Virtually all of the world's top female models are in their twenties. Some manage to make it into their thirties before they are "retired." Jeannine Stein is a writer who authored a column in the L.A. Times, cryptically entitled "Fashion Police." She quoted Heinz Holba, owner of L.A. models, who believes that the chances for a young person becoming a model are one in one million. For someone 40 years old, Mr. Holba puts the odds at becoming a model at one in 10 million.

Ford Models in New York includes what they call a "classic" division, reserved for models 35 and older. That division consists almost exclusively of models who have retained their looks as

Sean Connery

Sean Connery and Co-Star Catherine Zeta-Jones from the Movie *Entrapment*

they aged and have been with Ford since they were in their teens. In fact, older models almost always are made up of known commodities, women who made it when they were young.

I have concluded that an overwhelming number of women, no longer in their "prime," are psychologically poisoned each and every time an obviously aging and older man develops a sexual liaison with a young woman. Each and every time "the wife" of 25 years is traded in on a woman in her twenties, the toxic shock hits home. The match up is virtually always the same: older man with money takes up with younger, attractive female.

Getting older does not stop the quest for beauty, and all that goes with it. One of my 54-year-old research subjects, named Naomi, had been beguiled by her mother for years. Her mother had been beautiful as a young woman, and had never given into the aging process. My subject's mother was in her eighth decade of life before her health became a problem. As a result of those problems, Naomi was forced to have her mother cared for in a managed care facility. Naomi had lived a life of losing battle after battle with her mother on the dimension of beauty and all that goes along with it. The mother had flaunted her superior beauty at every opportunity. But alas, here was her mother in a managed care facility and the competition finally stopped; or did it? Shortly after Halloween, my research subject arrived for a follow-up meeting in tears. She reported that she had visited her mother at her nursing care facility and had come out of that meeting devastated, feeling unwanted and sexually unattractive. She brought with her a photograph of her mother. There she was, 88 years old, dressed like Cleopatra, from head to toe. It seems that dear old mom had flaunted the fact that she had the men in the retirement home eating out of her hand. "I've always had the edge with men," she bragged to her daughter. My research subject asked me if it ever ends. I told her that regretfully, no.

The prettier you are, if you are a woman, the worse the effects of aging on the psyche. Aging is the thief in the night who steals the beautiful woman's identity. It is not uncommon for the aging process to make the beautiful woman appreciate, for the first time in her life, that her popularity and identity are inextricably linked to her beauty. I have heard time and time again from aging beautiful women that they feel as though they lost their beauty overnight. One day, they just woke up and were no longer beautiful. What happened overnight was the realization. Realizations sometimes occur overnight. Seldom does one's beauty change in a 24-hour period.

The psychological maturity that comes from looking across a restaurant and seeing a 25–year-old beauty get all the looks is a make-or-break realization for the mostly ignored aging woman. The older woman, now ignored, actually sees herself 15 years earlier in the younger woman. The younger woman's abject ignorance about the difference between being a "that" and being a her, is balanced out at that exact moment when the difference becomes crystal clear to the aging woman. I reflect upon the U.S. Postal Service's poll, which asked Americans if they preferred the younger Elvis or the older, more mature Elvis. Was there ever any doubt?

Chapter VII: President William Jefferson Clinton

In 1997, a year before the public had ever heard of Monica Lewinsky and the impeachment of Bill Clinton, I was interviewed by a writer who had learned of my work in plastic surgery and beauty. The writer became interested in my fascination with Bill Clinton, or to be more precise, my fascination with the visceral hatred that some people expressed toward President Bill Clinton, and that hatred's relationship to beauty.

Bill Clinton's ability to solicit visceral hatred did, indeed, have an attractiveness connection. President Clinton is one of those men who women find to be attractive. While President Clinton was allegedly out fondling his way to an ever more popular standing in the polls, some men were left on the sidelines: less popular and almost by definition, less attractive. In an article that was to appear in a nationally known fashion magazine, I made note of Rush Limbaugh's notorious visceral hatred of President Clinton. (SEE PHOTO CREDITS OF RUSH LIMBAUGH) Mr. Limbaugh wasn't alone in his visceral hatred, which was shared by Congressmen Tom DeLay, Dan Burton and Dick Armey; and then Senator John Ashcroft, among others. (SEE PHOTO CREDITS OF TOM DELAY, DAN BURTON, DICK ARMEY AND JOHN ASHCROFT) I contrasted such hatred to other politicians who were diametrically opposed to President Clinton's policies and who probably did not like Mr. Clinton, but who did not express a visceral hatred for the President, such as Senators Fred Thompson and John Warner. The galleys had been set and my final edits made when an editor at the magazine pulled the article because it was, according to her, "too political and controversial." So much for good editorial judgment.

In studying this topic, it was rather easy to determine who vehemently hated Mr. Clinton, not only because his detractors could not keep their hatred a secret—their pursuit of the President was marked by teeth-gnashing hatred. Not since Jean Val Jean had anyone been pursued so fanatically as President Clinton. One of the more interesting characteristics about President Clinton's dogged pursuers, both men and women, is that as a group they struck me as significantly less attractive than were his supporters. But that wasn't the whole story. Besides being more unattractive as a group, they shared another characteristic, namely, they struck me as having a burning desire to be attractive and popular. I must stress that I am making a clear distinction between those who vehemently disagree with Bill Clinton's policies and those who viscerally hate him. It is the visceral hatred, not vehement disagreement, that betrays the unconscious forces at work, which is the focus of my treatise here.

Rush Limbaugh at Various Stages in His Life

Rush Limbaugh
Publicity Photograph

Rush Limbaugh
Jr. High School Photo 1968

Rush Limbaugh
Sr. High School Photo 1969

Representative Dan Burton

Attorney General John Ashcroft

Representative Dick Armey

Representative Tom Delay

Unflattering Depiction of
Congressman Tom DeLay

The attractiveness connection to the impeachment of the President involved relative unattractiveness paired with the desire to be beautiful, persuasive and popular. Unattractive women who had always wanted to be attractive, and who were jealous of those who were popular, were shrill in their visceral hatred of the President, while a number of more attractive women, those who did not emphasize their beauty, defended him with a competitive zeal.

One group of women hated President Clinton with unbridled venom. These women had all of the earmarks of those who had yearned to be beautiful when they were young. They craved to be popular like the pretty girls. It was quite ironic that their vocal hatred of the President gave many of them transient popularity, and placed them in the public eye. Many of these women, whose fifteen minutes of fame was inextricably linked to their vocal expression of hatred for the President, used the opportunity to make over their image, some going so far as to have cosmetic surgery. Instead of making themselves more beautiful and fulfilling their lifelong dream, they found themselves on the receiving end of a seemingly endless barrage of cruel satire regarding, of all things, and quite ironically, their looks.

Linda Tripp and Paula Jones are, perhaps, two of the most famous of President Clinton's detractors who underwent image makeovers, including cosmetic surgery paid for by President Clinton's political adversaries and enemies. (SEE PHOTO CREDITS OF LINDA TRIPP, PAULA JONES). The whole world could see their most recent makeover designed to make them beautiful. Instead, it added fuel to the already raging satirical fire which was intent upon consuming what was left of their self-esteem.

No matter how sophisticated the legal rationalizations voiced by Mr. Clinton's detractors, no matter how intricate the arguments involving violations of the rule of law, perjury or what have you, it was sex and attractiveness that was at the center of the emotional component of the impeachment motivation. President Clinton was not only more attractive to women than most of his peers, he was also more powerful. Power itself is a notoriously potent aphrodisiac. Add attractiveness and intelligence, and you have the trilogy of characteristics which can generate a visceral hatred from men and women who are highly reactive to the type of person President Clinton came to represent.(SEE CARTOONS FROM "RUSH LIMBAUGH, A HOMETOWN PAGE")

Let's not forget that sexuality was at the heart of Paula Jones' complaints against President Clinton. According to her, then-Governor Clinton made a rather overt sexual pass that offended her. That alleged act, alone, could not provide a legal remedy to her. Therefore, she bootstrapped that alleged boorish overture to allegations of hostility and retribution against her in the workplace for daring to reject the Governor's overtures. As Governor of Arkansas he was, technically, her boss.

Paula Jones' consultant and confidant, Susan Carpenter-McMillan, was herself a particularly vitriolic detractor of President Clinton who expressed any number of opinions on the subject

Content Found on
"Rush Limbaugh, a Hometown Page."
www.rosecity.net/rush/cartoons/

"YOU'RE A LIAR, CHARLIE BROWN. I WILL NOT DROWN IF YOU TAKE IT OUT"!!

"21...81...who cares! They can still bend over and get on their knees."

Linda Tripp and Monica Lewinsky

Linda Tripp
After Plastic Surgery

Source: Idleworm.com
One of the Many Unflattering Caricatures of
Linda Tripp

Paula Jones With Arkansas State Troopers

Susan Carpenter-McMillan (right)
with Paula Jones

Paula Jones
Before and *After*

of sexuality, ranging from pre-marital intercourse to abortion. Bill Maher, the host of the now defunct television show Politically Incorrect, asked Ms. Carpenter-McMillan the following question, the answer to which, once again, makes our précis here better than we could argue it: "If you could have sex with any famous person in history who would that be?" Mr. Maher asked. "President John F. Kennedy," answered Ms. Carpenter-McMillan, with a giddy smile. (SEE PHOTO CREDIT OF SUSAN CARPENTER-MCMILLAN WITH PAULA JONES) Linda Tripp was another woman who expressed a visceral hatred for President Clinton. Mrs. Tripp's notorious conversations with Presidential paramour Monica Lewinsky were all about sex. It was Monica whom President Clinton found to be sexually attractive, not Linda Tripp.

The impeachment of President Clinton, and the subsequent trial in the Senate, was a classic opportunity to study the link between political dogmatism and beauty. I should reiterate here that various and sundry vested interest groups were after the President for clearly defined partisan reasons. Moreover, many people were genuinely opposed to his administration's policies. Allow me to repeat that the merit of the attacks upon the President, or lack thereof, is not the subject of my discourse here. What I am referencing here is the source of the unbridled, *visceral* hatred of the President, above and beyond vehement dislike and disagreement with policies or political agenda.

To further investigate this phenomenon, I gathered two groups of women together in order to get their opinions on the matter. The two groups were made up of President Clinton's supporters, on the one hand, and on the other, his detractors. Both groups were matched for age and various socioeconomic factors. If there is no physical attractiveness effect operating on those who viscerally hate the President and those who support him, then attractiveness, as an independent variable, should be randomly distributed among both his supporters and detractors. Such was not the case.

A main effect was found where attractive women were more supportive of the President, compared to unattractive women. That effect was made even stronger when beauty was paired with the value given to physical beauty. Attractive women who were not focused upon their beauty were found to be significantly less critical of the President, than were unattractive women who also shared a burning desire to be beautiful. In the isolated instances where attractive women were found to be critical of the President, these women were likely to have grown up feeling they were unattractive, a feeling that persisted into adulthood. Unattractive women who were supportive of the President displayed little concern about their looks. Beauty, or the absence of it, was irrelevant to these women.

When the two groups of women were asked to evaluate four of the President's most vocal detractors, namely: Tom DeLay, Dan Burton, John Ashcroft and Dick Armey, the adjectives used to describe these men were quite different from the adjectives used to describe President Clinton, but shared a common nexus to sexuality.

The adjectives ascribed by President Clinton's supporters to Tom DeLay, Dan Burton, John Ashcroft and Dick Armey included nerdy, geeky and asexual. President Clinton's detractors ascribed the following adjectives to President Clinton: immoral, sexual pervert and adulterer. I draw the reader's attention to the common sexual thread which runs through both sets of adjectives used by attractive and unattractive women, respectfully. Unattractive women who had always yearned to be beautiful and popular fixated on the President's sexual promiscuity, while the more attractive women ascribed to the President's most vocal detractors adjectives which described their lack of sexual attractiveness.

To better understand the mechanisms involved here, our two groups of women were asked to evaluate two of the President's vocal, but not hateful, critics: Senators Fred Thompson and John Warner. Each man is reputed to be a charming conversationalist with a keen sense of humor. Fred Thompson's background includes a stint as a movie star of some stature, while John Warner was once married to none other than Elizabeth Taylor. Both of these men have impeccable conservative credentials, both vehemently disagreed with President Clinton on any number of issues, yet each man failed to express the visceral hatred felt by so many of their colleagues. Some would suggest that Senators Thompson and Warner are attractive to members of the opposite sex. Our research confirmed this impression. The group of women who supported President Clinton described our two conservative politicians as partisan, playing politics and petty, but men with whom they would probably enjoy having dinner, maybe even dating if their politics were different. Our relatively unattractive group of raters described Senators Warner and Thompson as men they would consider dating. None of these more conservative women expressed a desire to date Congressmen Burton, Armey, or DeLay, or then-Senator Ashcroft.

I am aware that my work here may be used by others to castigate, shame and satirize unattractive men and women who happen to be vocal critics of those who happen to be more attractive. This should be avoided. The origins of the visceral hatred toward attractive men begins, in part, with the unabated and cruel criticism heaped upon unattractive little boys and girls, beginning in grade school. Perhaps more important than outright criticism is the process of de-selection of these children by a culture that emphasizes beauty. They are also the product of a culture which equates physical attractiveness and popularity with self-worth and value.

Children most sensitive to and at risk for developing adult hatred toward the attractive are the little boys and girls who *crave* to be like their more popular, and almost by definition, more beautiful peers. Those same kids grow up to be talk-show hosts, senators, congressmen, governors, mayors and city counsel members. It is not uncommon for aspirations of power to be fueled, in part, by the compensatory mechanisms which derive from being de-selected as a child, and the need to compensate for those bad feelings. Insight into this phenomenon can benefit both the possessor of such hatred and those who conveniently and happily satirize them for not being pretty.

Presidential Looks

President Clinton's saga is but one example of how attractiveness can affect political behavior. President Richard Nixon recognized that his looks worked against him. In 1960, then-Vice President Richard M. Nixon debated then-Senator John F. Kennedy on television. Those who heard the debate on radio concluded that Mr. Nixon had won the debate. Those who saw the debate on television concluded that John Kennedy had won. Later in his career, Mr. Nixon lamented his physical unattractiveness and felt that he had suffered a number of prejudices throughout his life because of his looks. President Nixon declared to interviewer David Frost that no matter how much one may dislike it, you must listen to your image consultants when they offer suggestions to make you more attractive.

Former Vice President Dan Quayle was the target of relentless and often cruel commentary with regard to his intellect. What has received virtually no attention is the fact that Dan Quayle is a handsome man. The confluence of being attractive, while possessing an intellect that was arguably less than outstanding and holding a position of power, is the recipe for the hateful commentary and satire directed at Mr. Quayle. Vice President Quayle suffered from the "pretty boy" prejudice, just as President Nixon had suffered from the hateful "geek" prejudice.

Historically, Abraham Lincoln received often cruel and demeaning comments and was the object of hateful satire during his presidency, directed at his looks. More recently, during the Presidential election of 2000, women found Governor Bush to be more attractive than Vice President Al Gore.

The message is clear: if you are physically attractive and in politics, you had better be intelligent. If you are physically attractive, you'd better learn to resist sexual overtures and maintain a zero-threat persona to those who will inevitably be jealous and envious of you. If you are unattractive and in politics, you must be intelligent and charming. Given the demands of political life, it is clear that politicians can seldom steer clear of the troubles which come from the interaction of their looks, behavior and the prejudices of others.

Chapter VIII: Beauty Pageants

One of the more fascinating aspects of beauty pageants is that virtually everyone involved with pageants, including the contestants, deny that beauty is the driving force behind the pageant. This denial is stunning, considering that the events are called, after all, *beauty* pageants. Beauty is a four-letter word in the pageant business. (SEE MISS AMERICA WEB PAGE HEADER) But it wasn't always that way. Up until the 1960's, no one seemed to have a problem acknowledging the importance of "beauty" in beauty pageants. It was during that decade that feminists became particularly vocal in their criticism of judging beauty, especially within the context of a beauty pageant. One of the trends in the 1990's found women contestants who possessed neither beauty nor grace. This trend was a manifestation of the anti-beauty bias that had been heaped onto the pageant world by its most vocal critics. One of the more interesting aspects of this phenomenon is that the unattractive contestant's participation seems less political in its motive than a simple denial that beauty is still at the heart of the pageant world's raison d'être.

The internal workings of beauty pageants are as interesting as they are predictable. Miss Congeniality virtually never wins the pageant. (SEE PHOTO CREDITS OF MISS UNIVERSE 2001 AND MISS CONGENIALITY). The evening gown segment of the competition is invariably described as the most beautiful part of the pageant, but it pales in importance to the swimsuit part of the competition when it comes to the judge's ultimate decision, despite the fact that both are traditionally weighted equally. When it comes to the interview portion of the contest, its power resides in the fact that the interview portion of the pageant can ruin a contestant's chances of winning, but can seldom, in the absence of beauty, win the pageant for her. This is true despite the fact that the interview portion of the judging traditionally carries as much weight as the swimsuit and evening gown categories. The same is true for the contestant's on-stage interview. A contestant's on-stage answer to the host's impromptu question can ruin her chances of winning the crown, but cannot win the pageant for her, in the absence of beauty. No matter how good a contestant's answer is on stage or how well she conducted her interview, if she is not beautiful, her chances of winning are near zero. It should be noted that the Miss America pageant circuit includes a talent segment, whereas the Miss USA pageant circuit does not include a specific skill or talent as one of its categories upon which the contestant is judged. Over the years, the evolution of the talent portion of the Miss America pageant has witnessed the diminution of such things as baton-twirling to an ever-increasing number of women who display their musical and theatrical talents.

Web Site Header from the *Miss America* Web Page

"Miss Congeniality" Winner,
Miss Bahamas, Nakera Simms
Miss Universe Pageant 2001

Denise M. Quinones August
Miss Universe 2001

Miss Universe "Miss Style" Winner, *Miss Puerto Rico*, Denise M. Quinones August, *2001 Miss Universe Pageant*

Miss Universe "Best Swimsuit" Winner, *Miss Puerto Rico*, Denise M. Quinones August, *2001 Miss Universe Pageant*

Miss Universe "Miss Photogenic" Winner, *Miss Puerto Rico*, Denise M. Quinones August, *2001 Miss Universe Pageant*

Female judges, when compared to men, are the harshest critics for the contestants. I have witnessed over and over again the most beautiful girl in the pageant eviscerated by female judges who were so jealous of the beautiful contestant that they could barely contain their feelings. Vicious attempts to "trip" the contestant during her interview is the favorite pastime of the competitive female judge.

Over the years, the questioning during the interview process has become more and more political. Pageant directors try to limit "hot-button" issues such as religion and sex, but many judges insist on exploring such areas despite prohibitions to the contrary. Contestants sometimes use the interview process to express their own political or religious views. It may come as no surprise that those views, when expressed, are almost always conservative in nature. It is also interesting that certain interests, avocations and aspirations wax and wane in popularity. I remember that in the late 1980s and early 90s, being interested in the hearing impaired and American Sign Language was all the rage. Before that, women were universally, or so it seemed, interested in becoming news readers.

During the first group meeting, with all of the contestants present, the likely winners are identified by virtually all of the other contestants and pageant directors. Once this targeting occurs, the competition begins. The beautiful and intelligent contestant is the favorite target for the most competitive of her adversaries. She may, depending upon the particular pageant and its local director, be subjected to dirty tricks, psychological pressure, and blatant attempts to harm her reputation with the judges. Though very rare, judges report that attempts to influence their vote do occur. Most of the contestants play fair and enjoy the camaraderie afforded by the pageant experience.

Judges come from three general categories. The first category includes members of the pageant or beauty world. The second category includes public figures, and the third category includes benefactors. Judges usually attend a brief meeting wherein the do's and don'ts of judging pageants are outlined. But that is about it. Unless you have done it before, the new judge is left to his own devices. Judges are under a tremendous amount of pressure to not discuss the contestants with anyone, especially with other judges. For those readers who may be interested, sexual contact between judges and contestants is very rare…that is, until the pageant is over.

The family environment of beauty pageant contestants is affected by beauty. The more attractive the contestant, the more controlling the family environment. The relationship between mother and contestant is not infrequently permeated by an uneasy détente. With rare exception, beauty pageant daughters are significantly more attractive than their mothers, even when factors related to age and wardrobe are removed from the equation. In virtually every instance, the pageant contestant is the trophy of the family. She is the torch bearer for the family's self-esteem.

It may come as a surprise to many readers, but the vast majority of beauty pageant contestants are very bright. Many, in fact, have demonstrated one part of their intelligence with outstanding academic achievements. Predictably, however, each beautiful and bright contestant is typically subjected to intense criticism for the mere act of participating in a beauty pageant. Most of this criticism comes from women whose primary argument rests on the assumption that beauty pageants are exploitive of women. Ironically, the most vocal and articulate critics of beauty pageants are, themselves, significantly less attractive than the contestants they criticize. This pattern, in regard to the level of attractiveness of those who are most vocal in their criticism of beauty pageants, is replicated when we study those women who criticize the models who pose for Playboy. I do not mean to suggest that all of the women who criticize beauty pageant contestants are manifesting a form of "sour grapes." It may well be that in order to view any of the image businesses in a critical light, one must have been spared the intense and often addictive influences that come from being physically attractive. Perhaps as fascinating as the patterns found in those who criticize beauty pageant contestants, are the justifications that contestants make in response to these criticisms. Justifications for participating in a beauty pageant are virtually always linked to the economic empowerment that is provided by the pageant. Scholarships, stipends, travel opportunities and prizes are often offered as the justification, which counterbalances any alleged exploitation that may take place.

Pageant directors are, for the most part, very protective of the contestants. Directors shepherd the contestants through a maze of coming-of-age rituals within the pageant world that hopefully, if all goes well, becomes the director's personal legacy. Rather than competing with the beautiful contestants, like so many other women, the best directors share the contestant's beauty in a manner and style that is very similar to the fairy godmothers who "watched over" Sleeping Beauty.

Another Type of Beauty Pageant: Debutante Balls

Beauty pageants are cultural events that have a direct link to man's primitive past. Since time immemorial, humans have gathered the most beautiful women in the village to show off their charms to potential suitors. Beauty pageants share this cultural ritual with debutante balls. By comparing the debutante ball with the beauty pageant, much can be learned about the socio-biological meaning of pageants.

The English roots of the debutante ball extend back hundreds of years. In the United States, this ritual can be traced back to Colonial America. Debutante balls are usually limited to higher socioeconomic strata, and therefore are much less democratic, when compared to the more open beauty pageant world. Any beautiful woman from the community can enter a beauty pageant with hopes of winning; this is not so in the debutante world. The "deb" must already be a member of a certain social strata. Beauty pageant contestants are almost always made up of women from working class backgrounds who are both more beautiful and more intelligent than their families of origin. Debutante "contestants," on the other hand, are significantly less attractive than beauty pageant contestants on the whole. When compared to beauty pageant families, debutante families have more money and share the same level of attractiveness as their daughters. One must already be a member of the "club" before she can become the traditional debutante.

Debutantes, not infrequently, end up marrying men of equal social status. Beauty pageant winners, on the other hand, virtually always marry men of a higher social status. Beauty pageant winners, not infrequently, end up marrying men who saw them compete in the pageant or only know of them because they participated in the pageant. Debutantes, on the other hand, are already "known" because of their connections to their family of origin. In the instance of the beauty pageant, judges are gleaned from members of the community who possess a "special" status, e.g., doctors, media types, fashion experts, etc. In the debutante world, the men who show up to peruse the debutantes are hand-picked for their association to families of equal social status. In both "pageants," the idea is the same: present the young woman to her potential suitors. Needless to say, upward social mobility is more likely for the beauty pageant contestant than it is for the debutante.

In April of 2001, Nina Garin, writing for the San Diego Union Tribune, wrote the following in her coverage of a debutante ball named the "Ebony Pearl:" "To become a deb, the young ladies must have exceptional academic, athletic or volunteer records. The girls and their parents must be interviewed, plus, those dresses and classes don't come cheap. This year, 40 girls applied to be Ebony Pearls, 30 were accepted and 28 made it all the way." Garin noted that the debs take what are called "enhancement" classes, where they learn everything from leadership and public speaking skills to fashion and makeup techniques. They also meet for dance rehearsal on Saturdays.

The denial characteristic of the beauty pageant makes its way into the debutante world as well. Garin wrote: "The girls are aware that debs are often associated with spoiled upper-class girls. An average parent will spend from $1,000 to 2,000 on such things as classes, clothes, [and] invitations." Garin went on to quote one of the Ebony Pearl debs, who reportedly said, "They think it's all about money but it's not at all like that." Well, it isn't all about money; it is about a reproductive ritual. It just so happens that debutante ball pageants, unlike the more egalitarian and working class ritual of beauty pageants, are more controlled and influenced by money than looks alone, though beauty is a dominant factor in both.

Famous Pageant Winners and Contestants

Pageants have become more and more a form of show business. In addition to winning scholarship money and achieving upward social mobility, winning a pageant is frequently viewed as an entrée into show business, and not without reason. Oscar-winning actress Halle Berry's pageant titles include Miss Ohio-USA and first runner-up to the 1986 Miss USA Pageant. She also was fourth runner-up in the Miss World Pageant of that same year. Before that, she held the title of Miss

Teen All-American. Recording star and actress Vanessa Williams won the Miss America Pageant. She won both the talent and swimsuit portions of the competition. News woman Diane Sawyer won the title of America's Junior Miss. Oprah Winfrey held the titles of Miss Fire Prevention and Miss Black Tennessee. Sharon Stone competed in and won Saegertown's Spring Festival title, along with the Miss Crawford County crown in Pennsylvania. In addition to this group, the following women competed in pageants: Michelle Pfeiffer, Cloris Leachman, Paula Zahn, Delta Burke, Raquel Welch, Susan Anton, Marla Maples, Deborah Norville, Loni Anderson, Ali McGraw, Mary Hart and a host of others not so famous, but successful in any number of endeavors which puts them in contact with the public. Many of these women have publicly acknowledged that they learned something about performing and stage presence by competing in pageants.

Perhaps one can gain a fuller appreciation of the scope of the beauty pageant world by perusing the number of active websites currently maintained by various beauty pageant organizations. This list is by no means all-inclusive, but is representative of the popularity of beauty pageants as of the year 2002.

America's Junior Miss

America's Junior Miss

Alabama's Junior Miss

Alaska's Junior Miss

California's Junior Miss

Delaware's Junior Miss

Florida's Junior Miss

Kentucky's Junior Miss

Louisiana's Junior Miss

Massachusetts' Junior Miss

Michigan's Junior Miss

Missouri's Junior Miss

Ohio's Junior Miss

Oklahoma's Junior Miss

Oregon's Junior Miss

Tennessee's Junior Miss

Texas' Junior Miss

Virginia's Junior Miss

Washington's Junior Miss

Miss America

Miss America

Miss America History Page

Pressplus Miss America Archives

Miss Alabama

Miss Arizona

Miss Gilbert County

Miss Graham County

Miss California

Miss Hollywood and South Coast Counties

Miss Delaware

Miss District of Columbia

Miss Florida

Miss Georgia

Miss Blue and Gold

Miss Georgia Southern University

Miss Idaho

Miss Illinois

Miss Indiana

Miss Kansas

Miss Kentucky

Miss Southeast Kentucky

Miss Louisiana

Miss Maryland

Miss Tidewater

Miss Michigan

Miss Monroe County

Miss Minnesota

Miss Mississippi

Miss Missouri

Miss Nebraska

Miss New Hampshire

Miss Capital Area

Miss New Jersey

Miss New Mexico

Miss Quay County

Miss North Carolina

Miss North Dakota

Miss Ohio

Miss Greater Columbus

Miss Oklahoma

Miss Oregon

Miss Pennsylvania

Miss Berks County

Miss Central Pennsylvania

Miss Greater Juanita Valley

Miss Greater Lehigh Valley

Miss Susquehanna Valley

Miss York County

Miss Rhode Island

Miss South Carolina

Miss Charleston Southern University

Miss Greater Greenwood

Miss South Dakota

Miss Texas

Miss Auburn University

Miss Ellis County

Miss Hill Country

Miss Piney Woods area

Miss Southeast Texas

Miss Utah

Miss Utah Valley State College

Miss Vermont

Miss Virginia

Miss Blue Ridge Mountains Festival

Miss Hampton Holly Days

Miss Lonesome Pine

Miss Northern Virginia

Miss Washington

Miss West Virginia

Miss Wisconsin

Miss Northeast Wisconsin

Miss Wyoming

Miss Universe

Miss Universe

Miss Belgium

Miss Belize

Miss Brazil (unofficial)

Miss Chile

Miss Colombia

Miss Croatia

Miss Estonia 1998

Miss Estonia (English)

Miss Germany

Miss Hong Kong

Miss India

Miss Italy

Miss Lebanon

Miss Korea

Miss Mexico

Miss Paraguay

Miss Peru

Miss Poland 1996

Miss Poland 1997

Miss Puerto Rico

Miss Slovak Republic

Miss Sweden 1998

Miss Sweden (history)

Miss Switzerland

Miss Thailand

Miss Trinidad & Tobago

Miss Turkey

Miss US Virgin Islands

Miss Venezuela

Miss USA and Teen USA

Miss USA and Teen USA

Miss Arizona USA and Teen USA

Miss El Paso USA and Teen USA (TX)

Miss Florida USA and Teen USA

Miss Georgia USA and Teen USA

Miss Idaho USA

Miss Illinois USA and Teen USA

Miss Indiana USA and Teen USA

Miss Iowa USA and Teen USA

Miss Louisiana USA and Teen USA

Miss Montana USA and Teen USA

Miss Nevada USA and Teen USA

Miss North Carolina USA and Teen USA

Miss New York USA and Teen USA

Miss Ohio USA and Teen USA

Miss Pennsylvania USA and Teen USA

Miss South Carolina USA and Teen USA

Miss Virginia USA and Teen USA

Miss West Virginia USA and Teen USA

National Pageants

All American Girl & Boy Pageant

Miss American Beauty Pageant

American Doll Pageant

Audition '98

Miss Chinatown U.S.A.

C300: Pageant (Miss Toyota Grand Prix of Long Beach)

Holiday Angels

Miss Fitness America

Miss India Hong Kong

National Jewel USA Pageant

1998 Elegance Productions

Sunburst Beauty Pageant

Super Kids USA Pageant

Miss Wheelchair America Pageant

Mrs/Ms

Mrs. Ohio United States

Mrs. America Pageant

International Pageants

Miss Tourism World

Radiance World Beauty Pageant

Miss World Internet

MS. America Inter-Nationale Pageant

Mrs. Globe Pageant

(Source: Denise' Official Pageant Web Page-Links
www.geocities.com/Broadway/Stage/4217/index.html)

Chapter IX: Wardrobe

Wardrobe and our desire to present a beautiful image to others are inextricably linked. Once clothes with functional utility, such as outerwear in the Arctic, have been omitted from the designer's equation, clothes either enhance existing beauty, hide flaws or combine these two purposes. Even clothes which function as explicit uniforms, like police or military uniforms, incorporate designs which enhance beauty. Fashion designers are almost exclusively dedicated to the singular purpose of making the wearer of their clothes more noticeable, more alluring and more beautiful. One thoughtfully designed article of clothing brings together all the elements of fashion design that makes it both an art and a science.

Wardrobe is big business. Take, for example, the world's premier fabric show, the *Premier Vision*, a biannual affair displaying the best fabric in the world. During a typical four-day period, 40,000 visitors convene from around the globe just to look at fabric. At the exhibition you find somewhere around one and one-half million swatches manufactured by over 800 mills and from 14 countries. All of this material, in 1999, was displayed in a 42,000 square foot plant at the Parc d'Expositions de Paris, a convention complex near the Charles De Gaulle Airport. It is no wonder that such an exposition exists. In the year 2000, Americans spent approximately $300 million *per day* on clothes.

The wardrobe business is made up of niches, e.g., the teen, maternity, uniform or sports-related markets, just to name a few. Color, line, cut, print and texture are manipulated by the designer to achieve the wardrobe's beautifying effect for each niche in the business. When clothes make the wearer feel more attractive, it achieves that effect by changing the wearer's sense of self. In that respect, wardrobe shares that characteristic with cosmetic surgery. One type of garment that particularly affects our sense of self is the swimsuit.

Swimwear

A swimsuit embodies every hope, dream and fear of the woman who wears it. The swimsuit is a designer's nightmare. It is one thing to design a flowing dress that is easy to get lost in. It is quite another to design a swimsuit that a woman with less than a perfect body will feel comfortable wearing in public. Women are never more conscious of their bodies than when wearing a swimsuit. Absent cover-up accessory garments, the swimsuit has to do a lot of camouflaging with very little material.

The camouflaging motive in swimsuit design can be seen in the fact that seven out of ten women own a black swimsuit; that's because black slims and hides a multitude of beauty-sapping flaws. How many women feel comfortable baring most of their body for public consumption? One measure might be found in how many women dare to wear a thong swimsuit. Only eight percent of women own a thong swimsuit. Swimsuit models are notorious for having the best bodies in the modeling business. An interesting fact, given that virtually all women conclude that they would never look that good in a swimsuit when perusing fashion magazines. The fact is, size 12 is the most common size for a swimsuit, certainly not the size worn by swimsuit models.

Clothes' ability to impact our internal sense of beauty is never more clearly illustrated than in the instance of the undergarment. Despite what advertisers would have us believe, the vast majority of us never show our underwear, at least not completely. Just knowing that you are wearing sexy lingerie is enough to make many women feel sexy. Underwear has been the battleground for any number of cultural upheavals, and illustrates that wardrobe reflects a society's values about any number of issues, in addition to affecting our internal sense of self.

A Brief History of the Undergarment in America

Underwear has an interesting connection to beauty and culture. In the 1920's, women shed 200 years of fashion servitude by getting rid of the symbolic garment of that servitude, the corset. While women were ridding themselves of the corset, the Cadole company of Paris was busy developing something they called the "breast girdle." In the 1920s, when women got rid of their corsets, they immediately substituted exercise and dieting as a way to achieve the shape the corset had given them, and displaced their attention from the corset to the bra. Warner standardized the concept of "cup" size in 1935, and the first underwire bra was developed in 1938. In 1943, none other than Howard Hughes, himself, designed the bra worn by Jane Russel in the movie "Outlaws." This push-up bra gave its wearer a distinctive edge when it came to shape. In 1950, the first official bust-enhancing bra made by Maidenform sold 90 million units. The name of the company stands as a testament to the underlying dynamics of why this bra sold so many units. To fully appreciate just how large that number is, keep in mind that in 1950 the population of the United States totaled only 152 million people.

The most popular bra of all time, the "Cross Your Heart" Playtex bra of the sixties, withstood the women's movement effort to minimize the import of the bra for its wearers. When bras were burned in the 1960's, the breast became even more eroticized. Rather than liberating women, what soon followed was a boon in breast enhancement surgery and a continuous evolution in fashion leading to the "Wonder Bra" of 1994, where one unit was sold every 15 seconds shortly after the bra was introduced.

The corset of the twenties and the bra of the sixties were symbolic expressions of a retreat from an obsessive quest for beauty. Each withdrawal was short-lived, and followed by an even greater obsession with beauty. Nothing that men wear even comes close to the import of the bra. It may be true that Frank Sinatra padded the derriere in his sailor's outfit worn in the 1949 movie "On the Town," and that men's underwear is becoming more fashionable, but regardless of the importance of men's briefs, just remember that 75 percent of all men's underwear is still purchased by girlfriends, wives and/or mothers.

Corsets, bras, girdles and any other garment's raison d'être derives from its ability to enhance beauty. This is what Fredrick Mellinger knew when he developed undergarments that made movie stars look better on screen than they did in real life. Today, Mr. Mellinger's store, Fredrick's of Hollywood, and others like Victoria's Secret as well as all the other purveyors of wardrobe prestidigitation, all strive to create a feeling of sexual attractiveness in their customer's mind. As already mentioned in our chapter on *The Cult of the Beautiful Egg*, all types of women are buying risqué undergarments as we enter the new millennium.

Beauty isn't the only factor motivating the buyer, and beauty isn't the only internal psychological factor impacted by the designer. People buy clothes because of the feeling of belonging that some clothes are able to impart upon the wearer. This can best be seen in the sports wardrobe market. The clothes that fit into this category are emblazoned with professional sports team insignias, logos, colors, mascots, jersey numbers and even facial images of particular athletes. Absent logos, these garments fall into the casual clothes niche. Add something to casual wear that gives the wearer a sense of belonging, and sales dramatically increase. What follows illustrates the point.

It is estimated that three out of five adult Americans purchase sports merchandise related to football, baseball, basketball or hockey teams each year, with the majority of those items wardrobe related, e.g., T-shirts, jackets, sweatshirts, etc. Consumers spend an average of $232 dollars on team-related sports merchandise every year. Almost equal proportions of men and women have purchased team related goods, with men typically spending more than women. Among young adults ages 18 to 24, it is estimated that 66 percent have purchased sports merchandise. 69 percent of those between the ages of 25 and 30 have purchased sports related products. (Source: Harris Poll of 1,009 adults surveyed between September 9 and 13, 1998) The *Licensing Letter*, which tracks sports related merchandise licensing fees, reported revenues for the year 2002 as follows: Major League Baseball, 2.7 billion; National Football League, 2.5 billion; National Basketball Association, 1.6 billion; NASCAR, 1.2 billion; and the National Hockey League, .9 billion.

Another less specific type of belonging can also be expressed by wardrobe. This involves designer labels. Parents with middle-school age children understand the power of Nike basketball labels emblazoned on their children's shoes. The Gucci insignia, along with a host of other designer icons, tell all who care to notice that the wearer of these clothes is "special." "Who are you wearing?" is the oft-heard question asked of celebrities who walk the red carpet at such events as the Oscars or the Cannes Film Festival. The question that arises is: what is it that makes the wearer of such designer labels special? And to what does the wearer of such clothes belong? After all, anyone can buy designer clothes, that is, if they can afford it. And therein is the nexus to that which connotes specialness. Designer label clothes tell others that you belong to an exclusive sociodemographic group that can afford to purchase designer-label clothes. Nieman-Marcus, Sachs and a host of other exclusive department stores tap into this elite class-belonging phenomenon.

As we have already seen, culture is reflected in wardrobe and vice versa. Pop music culture offers a good example of the relationship. The fans of pop music stars strive to make themselves physically resemble the objects of their affection on stage. Audience members, reacting to the wardrobe of pop music stars, alter their appearance to match the musicians as both a way of tapping into the star's cache and as a way of expressing an identification with the star. Fashion trends, which often begin with those in the music business, generate millions upon millions of dollars worth of revenue for the fashion industry. These trends often begin with the fans and eventually filter down to permeate society as a whole.

Pop music stars can change the look of an entire generation. For example, Elvis' turned-up collar not only became the rage in 1957, but anyone who peruses the scores of 50-something golfers with their golf shirt collars turned up à la Elvis is forced to make the connection. The Beatles' effect on hair style; Madonna's layered look, which included wearing her underwear as an outer layer; Britney Spears' exposed midriff, which helped to bring back "hip-hugger" pants first popularized in the 1970's; the Sex Pistols, who created the look we have come to call the "punk" look; or the "hip-hop" culture's ubiquitous fashion statement of baggy pants, oversized shirts and distinctive footwear, that not only defined the look of inner-city youth but their anglo-suburban soul mates as well; are all classic examples of this phenomenon. Russell Simmons has made a fortune selling hip-hop style clothes under his brand name of *Phat Farm*. Sean "Puffy" Combs has done the same.

The reader who may be reading this book at some point in the future, need only substitute "their" generation's music stars for the above listing. Nothing else will change, and all of the principles will remain the same. The reactions of the men and women who constitute the audiences in the pop music business are remarkably the same across generations. If it were not for differences in wardrobe, makeup, hairstyle and other visual cues affecting current definitions of beauty, it would be very difficult to tell one audience from another without listening to the music itself. Women cry, scream, wring their hands and engage in a pseudo-group sexual experience in remarkably similar ways from one generation to another. Each member of that same hysterical audience, however, is deluded into thinking that their experience is unique and somehow related to them as individuals and the music idols they adore, as opposed to what it really is: an exact replica of a timeless phenomenon, with the only variation being what constitutes beauty when it comes to the "look" of a generation.

John Malloy's book "Dress for Success," and an almost endless listing of other treatises on wardrobe, promise its readers that they, too, can influence people to their financial betterment by how they dress. This idea has so permeated American culture that virtually everyone knows what color designates the so-called "power tie." Enter a courtroom on the first day with jurors present, and the number of blue suits and red ties is mind-boggling. Featured speakers at multi-level marketing seminars love the red "power tie."

The dress-for-success movement became so popular that in the 1990's, a new movement toward casual dress infiltrated the business market. The notion behind the power of casual wear is that truly powerful people can afford to dress in flannel shirts with Khaki pants. This phenomenon toward casual made its way into presidential politics in full force in the 1980's, where candidates indulged in the now-obligatory casual-wear photo shoot. The idea is that by dressing like their constituents, the voter will conclude that the candidate is "one of us." Since everyone now seems to understand how clothes are used to influence others, a backlash has occurred when the attempt to exercise power over others with wardrobe is suspected.

What remains when the manipulative motives behind wardrobe are removed once again reminds us of the importance of beauty. Clothes that make the wearer more attractive by using subtle and classic designs will never go out of style. The key is to appear attractive without eliciting reactance from others. Good taste has always been in short supply when it comes to wardrobe. The distinction between fad and fashion is not an easy one to make, and cannot be bridged by designer labels, Machiavellian motives to influence others, or an unlimited budget.

Chapter X: Murderous Rage

When JonBenet Ramsey was murdered, lots of people asked my opinion on the subject. I was asked partly because of my work in forensics and partly because of my experience with beauty pageants. What I was not asked about was the obvious fact that this little victim, like so many victims before her, was a beautiful victim. JonBenet was only one of over 900 children under the age of ten who were murdered in 1996. But she was beautiful; a beauty pageant contestant. (SEE PHOTOS OF JONBENET RAMSEY FROM *PEOPLE MAGAZINE* AND THE RAMSEY FAMILY WEB PAGE)

What nobody seems to notice, except beautiful women, is that beauty makes its owner a target. The murderers of countless beautiful kids and adults undoubtedly focused upon the beauty of their victim. What is it about beauty that can generate murderous rage? In the instance of Selena's murderer, Yolanda Saldivar was a 35-year-old registered nurse from San Antonio who quit her job to become president of the Selena fan club and devote herself to managing the star's boutiques…that is, until she murdered Selena. (SEE PHOTO CREDITS OF SELENA AND YOLANDA SALDIVAR)

When Robert John Bardo killed Rebecca Schaeffer, it was not coincidental that he killed a beautiful woman. (SEE PHOTO CREDIT OF REBECCA SCHAEFFER FROM *SEVENTEEN MAGAZINE*) It was her beauty, after all, that entranced him, attracted him and predictably, rejected him. In the attempted murder trial known as the "cheerleader's mom" case, the intended victim was someone prettier than the would-be murderer's daughter. When Tanya Harding involved herself in the assault on Nancy Kerrigan, it was, once again, unattractive assaulting beauty.

This pattern in human behavior has manifested in our fairy tales. Take a good look at Maleficent, then take a good look at Princess Aurora. You may know Princess Aurora by her more popular name, Sleeping Beauty. The Wicked Queen from Snow White was obsessed with asking the question: "Mirror, mirror on the wall, who is the fairest of them all?" What happens when you repeatedly ask that question, and the mirror repeatedly gives you the name of someone else? Take a good look at Cinderella and compare her to her sisters on the dimension of beauty. Pay close attention to the attractiveness of the Wicked Queen as she consults her mirror. (SEE PHOTO CREDITS OF CINDERELLA, HER SISTERS AND THE WICKED QUEEN).

JonBenet Ramsey's murderer, unknown as of the writing of this book, both loved and hated the little girl. As I have written elsewhere, "beautiful women are the women we *love* to *hate*." Who could hate a little girl? If the child, in the murderer's mind, was inseparable from her beauty, then

A Glamorous JonBenet Ramsey on the Cover of *People Magazine*

JonBenet Ramsey
From the Ramsey Family Web Page.
Note the Absence of Glamour Photographs

Selena's Gravestone

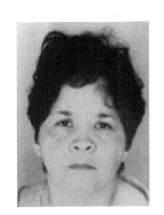

Yolanda Saldivar, Convicted
Killer of Selena

Selena Promotional Photo

Yolanda Saldivar as She
Looked in Court

Rebecca Schaeffer on the Cover of *Seventeen Magazine*

"CINDERELLA TRIED TO MAKE HER SISTERS LOOK AS WELL AS POSSIBLE."
by
Margaret Evans Price

Cinderella. Edited by Katharine Lee Bates. Cover and Color Illustrations by Margaret Evans Price. Originally Published by *Rand McNally & Company*, Chicago:1921.

Disney Illustration

Cinderella's Sisters and Step-Mother

"My sash!" cried Drizella.
"My beads!" cried Anastasia.
They ripped off the sash and
pulled off the beads. Cinderella's
dress was ruined.

Disney Illustration From
Walt Disney's *Wonderful
World of Reading*

Cinderella and Her Step-Sisters

Disney Illustration

"Mirror Mirror on the Wall, Who is the Fairest of Them All?"

eradicating the beauty and the bad feelings it created came at the cost of killing the child. JonBenet was an innocent victim who had to die if beauty was to die. If a woman killed JonBenet, she was killed, in part, because of the rage generated by jealousy at someone who had what the murderer had wanted more than anything in her own life. If the murderer was a male, the murderer most likely fell in love with beauty and repressed the fact that such beauty resided in a little girl. Sexually acting out attraction to beauty, when its possessor is a little girl, suggests to the perpetrator that beauty must die if his assault is to remain hidden.

Beauty is a marketable commodity, and men like Indle Gifford King Jr. know where to look for it. In March of 2002, Mr. King was sentenced to 28 years and 11 months in prison for killing his mail-order bride, a beautiful young blond named Anastasia. This was King's second beautiful mail-order bride. His first wife has filed for divorce from King, which cost him $55,000 and a lot of heartache. Both his first and second mail-order brides had found King to be controlling and abusive.

At the sentencing hearing, Anastasia's father, Anatolyi Soloviev, told King, "You weren't getting yourself a wife, you were getting yourself a doll. You wanted to go around and show off your young bride, show everybody how successful you were." King had killed Anastasia with the help of a boarder in the Kings' home in the north Seattle suburb of Mountlake Terrace. The boarder, Daniel Larson, testified that he strangled Anastasia with a necktie while her 270-pound husband sat on top of her. This phenomenon is so widespread, and is beginning to be recognized for its threat to beautiful women, that in March of 2002, Governor of Washington Gary Locke signed a law, the first of its kind in the USA, which requires mail-order bride companies to give brides-to-be the criminal and marital histories of their prospective Washington spouses.

In May of 2003, a homely man by the name of Robert J. Ambrosino shot and killed his girlfriend, Lyric Benson. Lyric was an up-and-coming actress, recognized for her beauty. Ambrosino shot her in the face when she tried to leave him. One of the couple's friends, Chelsea Lagos, said of Ambrosino and Benson: "The one thing that everybody would say when they met them, anytime, anyone, anywhere, was, 'What's she doing with him? She was just in a different league.'" Shaila K. Dewan, a writer for the New York Times News Service, covered the story and wrote the following: "Bobby Ambrosino, from upstate New York, could not match her beauty—he had a slight frame and, in self-deprecating words recalled by a friend, 'a face like a catcher's mitt.'" (SEE PHOTO CREDITS OF INDLE GIFFORD KING AND MAIL-ORDER BRIDE; ROBERT J. AMBROSINO AND LYRIC BENSON)

What do Jonesboro, Arkansas, Springfield, Oregon, Paducah, Kentucky, Moses Lake, Washington, Pearl, Mississippi, Littleton, Colorado and Santee, California have in common? They are all locations where disenfranchised teenage boys, called geeks, gangly, skinny, dorks and/or ugly, have gone on a murder spree against their more attractive and popular classmates and teachers. In

Associated Press

Indle Gifford King Jr. is Shown in Seattle with His
Late Mail-Order Bride Anastasia King, in 1998

New York Times

Robert J. Ambrosino and the Late Lyric Benson

the instance of Littleton, two boys named Eric Harris and Dylan Klebold went after the popular boys and some pretty girls. Fifteen were killed in that rampage. Eric and Dylan were described by their classmates as skinny, gangly and ugly. In one news report following the Littleton massacre, one classmate was interviewed who reported that she had been asked by one of the boys to ask a girl to the prom on his behalf. The girl being interviewed said that when she asked, the girl just laughed. (SEE PHOTOS OF ERIC HARRIS AND DYLAN KLEBOLD)

On March 24, 1998, in Jonesboro, Arkansas, Andrew Golden and Mitchell Johnson, two other boys called ugly, took aim at their classmates: four girls and a teacher. The girls were pretty. The murders in Paducah, Kentucky were committed by a boy named Michael Carneal, who was called a geek and a nerd by his fellow classmates. Barry Lewkitis, a 14–year-old boy who others called a dork, killed two students and a teacher in February of 1996 at Frontier Jr. High in Moses Lake, Washington. "He asked me out a couple of times. I refused," said one of his female classmates during his trial. Barry was picked on relentlessly. Manuel Vella Jr., the most popular boy in Barry's junior high school, was Barry's target. Just a few months later in Pearl, Mississippi, Luke Woodham targeted the girl who had jilted him. Luke wrote in his diary: "I killed because people like me are mistreated everyday." Luke is an unattractive boy who was a convenient target for abusive kids. Kip Kinkel, a tortured and unattractive kid, included his parents in his vengeful murder spree in Springfield, Oregon.

Charles "Andy" Williams, a 15 year-old Freshman at Santana High School, in Santee, California who, according to press reports at the time, was a skinny kid who was the butt of jokes and was routinely picked on, killed two classmates and wounded 13 others on March 5, 2001. Terry McCarthy, writing for Time Magazine in its March 19, 2001 issue, quoted Gentry Robler, a 16 year-old sophomore at Santana High School, who said that, "This is a school that was waiting for something like this to happen." McCarthy then went on to write in his article: "But who would have guessed that it would be the skinny, jug-eared timid freshman wearing a silver necklace with the name MOUSE on it? Who would make this happen? Perhaps a better question is: "Who wouldn't have guessed?" (SEE PHOTO OF ANDY WILLIAMS)

Buford Furrow, the man who admitted shooting 5 people, including children, at a Jewish community center North of Los Angeles in 1999 was, according to the descriptions of former classmates, a bespectacled, ugly and nerdy kid. The hatred generated by forced pariah status, like an electrical charge in a thunderhead, discharged onto innocent children. The profoundly stupid choice of where to project hatred often overshadows the search for the genesis of the hatred in the first place. Hatred, spawned by one's tendency to be rejected by others, antedated his feelings about any one group.

Hate groups are made up almost exclusively of men who as children and young adults are lacking in charm, intelligence, social skills and yes, physical attractiveness. The normal variances

Eric Harris and Dylan Klebold, Killers of Their Classmates Caught on Surveillance Video
During Their Killing Spree in Littleton, Colorado

Andy Williams, Admitted Killer of His Classmates at Santana High School
Located in Santee, California, in 2001

in beauty found in society at large are not found within hate groups. The bell curve is skewed toward the unattractive end of the beauty distribution. Social charm is also missing within these groups. We see a profile of the members of hate groups who, without any other traits or characteristics available to counterbalance their unattractiveness, become filled with anger and hate.

Predictably, every warning sign in the world is targeted by the pundits, who pop up like mushrooms after a warm summer rain, after one of these now-ritual tragedies occurs. They never seem to focus on the rage which emanates from the one thing all of these killers have in common: they are physically unattractive, yet crave to be otherwise. These people hate, with a passion, anyone who treats them badly. These kids hate, with ferocity, their life.

None of the pundits seem capable of ferreting out one of the basic problems in science, "cause and effect." Thus, everything that these murderous children and adults do is mistaken as a cause of their rage, not as an expression of it. Their music, their dress, their "cliques," their internet activities, etc., are classified as causes. In the same press reports which carry the story, if you look just a bit closer you begin to understand the deeper story.

For instance, in a large Southern California newspaper it was written about the Littleton murders: "Two struck pose of rebels but were seen as losers." In the same paper, on the same day, another lead story about a high school event was captioned this way: "School's annual fashion show is tribute to grid hero who died." In another example, one of the major television networks faded to black just after an expert on teen culture gave his opinion about violent music as one of the causes of teen rage. The commercial that immediately ran showed a handsome male trying on a pair of sunglasses in front of a mirror. Of course, the anchor on this program was, at least in part, chosen for her striking beauty before the camera. Every host on each and every one of these programs is coifed, bathed in flaw fighting light, made up, dressed and otherwise made to look better on camera than they do in person, and all the while these same men and women struggle to understand how unattractive high school kids could feel so alienated while regularly dosed with the ever-present, beautiful news reader.

Five years after the Michael Carneal shootings, reporters were still at a loss to explain his behavior, while their writings about the subject were replete with any number of adjectives which described Carneal's level of attractiveness. "Michael Carneal, a skinny freshman....He slouches into his chair in a conference room at the Kentucky State Reformatory in LaGrange...He is 19 years old now; tall, pudgy, pasty with a scraggly beard and chunky square glasses. It's hard to see in him the scrawny, skittish freshman who pulled out a .22-caliber Ruger, pressed foam plugs in his ears and opened fire that Monday morning."

One of Carneal's victims, Missy Jenkins, was quoted in this particular newspaper article describing herself to others: "My name is Missy Jenkins. I had a GPA of 3.3. I was homecoming queen runner-up. I was vice president of my junior class. I was shot by a classmate." For Carneal's part, he offers no explanation for why he did what he did, but he remarked: "I thought I might as well go to prison because I didn't have anything to lose."

In the pecking order of high school, the unattractive kids make up the "out" groups, with rare exception. Females relentlessly and ruthlessly "deselect" unattractive males. Some boys take to this better than others, but virtually all boys respond with hurt feelings, and some with hatred. Some boys displace that hatred and sublimate that negativity into other activities less violent. Others can't or won't.

Not all murderous rage ends in murder. Sometimes murderous rage is bridled, but never completely. Take Heidi Fleiss, for example. Before Heidi became the "madame to the stars," she worked for another woman named "Madame Alex." Madame Alex was the rather homely woman who turned the cute Heidi Fleiss in to the authorities. Madame Alex reportedly utilized her contacts at the L.A. Vice Squad to carry out her vendetta. While Heidi Fleiss had taken business from many other madames in L.A., none were as unattractive or vindictive as Madame Alex. The take-home message is, regardless of what form the anger takes, it is always present and manifests in some way. Sometimes that includes murder.

I will not make the same mistake that others do by citing physical unattractiveness as the sole cause of murderous rampages at schools across America. My point is that the unattractiveness factor has been all but ignored. Being unattractive gets you picked on, it isolates you and helps to make unattractive kids without coping skills a receptacle for unbelievable cruelty from some of their peers.

Others hate that which is unattractive, in part, because they are afraid of it in themselves. Some reasonably attractive kids pick on the ugly kids. Seldom do the truly beautiful children pick on unattractive kids. The truly beautiful kids have their own cross to bear, and as you can see, are often the targets of unattractive kids because of the fact that they are attractive. Our society in America is Spartan in its credo. We offer no mercy to those who feel left out. We create materialistic and cruel children who are obsessed with looks and status with deadly efficiency. We fuel the next school shooting with a culture that idolizes prom kings and queens, cheerleaders, jocks as role models and so-called school pride which idolizes the football hero. Competition is considered good, regardless of who is left out. The movies "Carrie" and "Never Been Kissed" are telling depictions of what children face in America's schools every day of the school year. It is not likely to change any time soon.

I've seen the unattractive's vendetta against the beautiful in every walk of life, and at every age. "Come here my pretty," said the Wicked Witch of the West. Everything about Dorothy was pretty, and everything about the Wicked Witch was ugly. It was, after all, the ugly sisters who hated Cinderella. It was the ugly queen, after all, who ordered that the poison apple be fed to the beautiful Snow White.

Chapter XI: Apples, Peaches, Pumpkin Pie

If you want to get a sense of the importance of beauty, pay attention to the sellers of this world. The sellers of cosmetic surgery and makeup understandably place a great deal of emphasis upon beauty. After all, it is beauty that they are selling. But take a look at the sellers of canned soup or automobiles, and you see the same thing: beauty and the attractiveness which comes from it can all be yours only if you eat this soup or drive this car. If you are lucky, if you buy the fancy car you can have the model who advertised it; or, if you are a woman, you can now have men tripping all over themselves just to say hello. That is the subliminal message: "You can have beauty if you buy my product."

Pity the poor praying mantis, I have yet to see one piece of cloisonné jewelry crafted in its image. On the other hand, consider the ladybug. Everywhere you look, you find not only cloisonné jewelry, but handbags, ash trays, wall stencils and countless other articles, all crafted in the image of the ladybug. The ladybug is an attractive, innocuous bug, while the praying mantis is an ugly, voracious insect which bites off the head of its mates, right? Actually, gardeners have a nickname for the ladybug: "Aphid Dragon." The ladybug hovers over aphids and sucks out their bodily fluids, ingesting its victims a drop at a time. Not exactly attractive behavior, wouldn't you agree? The fact remains that the ladybug is physically attractive, and the praying mantis is ugly. (SEE PHOTOS OF LADY BUG INSPIRED ARTIFACTS AND PRAYING MANTIS)

Makeovers are not reserved for people: we also do it to our fruits and vegetables. Oranges aren't perfectly orange. They come off the tree an admixture of green, orange and yellow. Some types of oranges are cultivated for their beautiful peels. We don't always find Mother Nature's coloring pretty, so we dye oranges a perfect orange. We buy pretty oranges; we don't buy the ugly ones. We wax cucumbers, polish apples and dye and polish countless other foods in order to make them pretty. The prettiest foods are also the most appetizing. A poor presentation can ruin an otherwise delectable meal. We choose our homes, our cars, our furniture and a host of other material items based upon their beauty.

Volvo is a wonderful case study in the power of beauty. For years, Volvo made cars that were engineered with an eye toward safety and utility. Beauty was not one of Volvo's priorities. While the Big Three American Auto Makers were manufacturing beautiful death traps, Volvo was producing safe, reliable and ugly cars.

All that changed in 1999. An ad for the 1999 Volvo S-80 read: "A California body with a Swedish soul inside." In 1999, an S-80 television ad began with the voice-over of a sultry woman

Ladybug Inspired Products

Praying Mantis

asking over and over: "How do I look, how do I look?" Volvo has gone to beauty school, a concession to the importance of beauty in a world which has found it more and more difficult to emphasize substance over form.

Apple Computer was in the dumps in 1997 when Steve Jobs, one of Apple's original founders, decided to produce a machine that was image-conscious. The iMac came in pastel colors with an egg-like shape that set it apart from all other computers. Apple's beautiful computer sold like hot cakes and, at the time, single-handedly turned Apple's waning fortune around. After Apple redesigned its iBook laptop computer in 2001, the following review appeared: "The same basic drive train as the old model, but a flashy new body." The review goes on: "But what a body. The old iBook was winsome but bulbous and bulky. Its replacement is angular and trim."

Turn on one of the television shopping channels and you'll see jewelry touted for its beauty right along with an ever-growing number of products designed to preserve, increase, create and promote beauty. Callers who speak with shopping channel hosts frequently begin their call with comments about how beautiful the host looks. "Beauty sells" is an axiom that nobody ever went broke following, and a lot of people have gotten rich by simply linking their product with pretty form or pretty people.

Function and design are almost always interrelated. Concessions to design at the expense of function provide the best examples of the importance of beauty. High-heeled shoes, long nails and tight pants are but a few examples of where function has been compromised to benefit image. Food dyes and packaging design have little, if anything, to do with the function or quality of the underlying product. Yet, unattractive foods don't sell and when shoppers peruse the aisles of foodstuffs at grocery stores, what they mostly see is attractive packaging. It is no wonder that in some instances, costs associated with the package are higher than the costs for producing the product within.

Chapter XII: Beauty and Substance

Comedian Jerry Seinfeld's standup routine includes the following remarks, and I paraphrase: "A person's looks don't impress anyone whose blind, but longer lasting, more substantial qualities do. If you ladies in the audience want to hit on a blind man, you'd better have something to say, and it better make sense." Seinfeld's satire on the subject forces one to ponder the fact that blind people, if they come to know you, almost always want to "feel" your face so that they can get a sense of how you look. Anecdotal evidence suggests that wealthy blind men often have beautiful girlfriends and wives.

Beauty and substance are naturally assumed to be mutually exclusive qualities. Beauty is on the outside and substance is on the inside, right? Talk about beauty and substance, and people naturally assume that these two elements are in a sort of zero sum relationship, i.e., the greater the beauty, the less substance is involved. And the converse is worth articulating: Really smart and meaningful people are not beautiful to look at, right?

Beauty and substance have a built-in gender factor. All is not necessarily rosy for men who are "just" attractive. Being "just" attractive if you are male virtually always means that you are not taken seriously. When you are "just" a beautiful woman you can be taken very seriously, not only professionally, but personally as well. The "just" beautiful woman can become the wife of a successful man, or she can make lots of money and be respected in any number of image-based endeavors. On the other hand, both men and women virtually always give the name "male bimbo" to "just" attractive men. The world is full of "pretty boys" who have no power, no money and who get no respect from either men or women.

As touched upon in our chapter on beauty pageants, there are special substance awards that are both designed to assuage the guilt associated with highlighting beauty and to recognize those women who, because of their relative absence of beauty, don't have a chance of winning the "beauty" pageant. Winners of essay awards, community service awards and the famous "Miss Congeniality Award," virtually never win the pageant. But is this because beautiful women are less substantive? Take, for example, the holder of the title 1999 Miss Thailand. This beautiful 24-year-old woman was as smart as she was beautiful. Apisamal Srirangsan, or should I say Dr. Apisamai Srirangsan, was Thailand's first beauty queen physician.

How did her peers deal with the beauty/substance equation? Nongpanga Limsuwan, a professor at Khon Kaen University in Thailand, has stated that a beauty queen cannot be a good psychiatrist, since patients can relate to her in an inappropriate way. At the Siriraj Hospital in

Bangkok, some doctors have said that they would never have allowed Dr. Apisamal to train there if they had known she was Miss Thailand. (SEE PHOTO CREDITS OF MISS THAILAND)

Siriporn Scrobanechy, a Secretary General of Thailand's Women's foundation, was quick to defend Miss Thailand when she stated that it is unfair that she should be branded for the rest of her life as a sexy girl who adores her own beauty too much. She can be something else, if she has enough talent. Most Thai beauty queens, like beauty queens from all over the world, end up as singers, models and actresses. These vocational "choices" are made for the beautiful woman, despite the fact that she may have talents and abilities that would take her into, for example, medicine. If you want to know why that doesn't happen with some regularity, take note of what has happened to Miss Thailand. Women psychiatrists and unattractive doctors can't allow it; they won't tolerate it without making Miss Thailand run the gauntlet. Such is the fate of beautiful women.

Nothing about being beautiful means that nature has denied you substance. We all are familiar with the doors that open to beautiful women, but for every door that opens, a door of substance closes. Consider that the modeling door de-emphasizes intellect. More fundamentally, the modeling door doesn't allow those inside to market themselves as substantive. In the same vein, the jealousy that is elicited by beautiful women who do make it into academic careers is horrendous.

The Ironies of Being Beautiful

Beautiful people typically do not focus upon beauty when it comes to companion animals. Unattractive people, on the other hand, often obsess upon having beautiful things. Beautiful people don't mind mutts from the pound. Unattractive people are more likely to go to breeders and buy the prettiest dog they can afford. I have studied the attractiveness of women at breeder's dog shows and I have similarly studied socially minded women who rescue strays and help adopt orphan animals. Just as the breeder's dogs are beautiful and their owners are not, the plain-looking dogs at the pound often have beautiful women trying to rescue them, whether it is Bridget Bardot, the late Tippi Hedron, Doris Day, Pamela Anderson-Lee, The "Barbi Twins" or Jilian Barbieri. A cursory review of beautiful actresses and models found them remarkably dedicated to the little unattractive and unfortunate orphan animals who, without their efforts, would be killed.

The logic which explains these findings suggests that beautiful women do not need an "ego companion creature" to make them feel good about the way they look. The beautiful woman doesn't need the beautiful fur of a slain animal to enhance her beauty. But what about those women who do? The desire to be beautiful can be compensated for in any number of ways. As we have discussed, the quest for beauty can manifest in requests for plastic surgery, becoming a cosmetic junkie or in "owning" a self object. A self object is a thing, creature or even another person, which represents a part of the owner's self. Thus, when an unattractive man drives a beautiful sports car,

Can You Pick Out the Physician in the Photo?

(Left to Right): Brenda Liz Lopez, *Miss Puerto Rico* 1999; Miriam Quiambo, *Miss Philippines,* 1999; Dr. Apisamai Srirangsan, *Miss Thailand,* 1999; Sofia Raptis, *Miss Greece,* 1999

(Photo From the *Clairol Herbal Essences Style Award Seminar* for the 1999 *Miss Universe Pageant Contestants.* May 13, 1999, Trinidad and Tobago)

Dr. Apisamai Srirangsan

he feels better about himself. He *is* the sports car. By owning a special breed of dog, beautifully coifed and pretty, the owner becomes special, regardless of their personal level of attractiveness.

There is an old saying about the women on New York City streets: "The models look like secretaries and the secretaries look like models." Truly attractive people welcome the respite that comes from playing down their beauty. Truly unattractive people are obsessed with the issue and won't allow themselves to be seen, ever, in an unattractive light.

Sexuality

Beautiful women have access to a seemingly endless supply of potential sexual partners, or so the myth goes. Studies seem to show that beautiful women are fun to date but that men may not necessarily want to marry them. It is also true that beautiful women have more men in their lives, but not necessarily because that is the way beautiful women want it. Researchers report that beautiful women have more, but shorter relationships. From the beautiful woman's perspective, a new beau who is overwhelmed with your beauty is a refreshing change from your last lover, who may have grown tired of your most salient trait.

Beautiful women can be smart, kind, talented, strong or rich, but it is beauty that is their dominant trait. It is the one trait that is immediately visible and understood by everyone. It is the one trait that is universally valued. It is the one trait that will get a woman the most attention for the least amount of effort.

Anecdotal data suggest that beautiful women may not be considered very good lovers. They are often described as relatively unresponsive, when compared to average or unattractive women. Theories abound to explain these impressions. The most logical is that beautiful women have learned that they do not need to be particularly skilled and/or responsive. But of course, this only becomes a problem when, over time, men tend to habituate, or get used to, their beautiful partner, and come to desire someone who is responsive.

Youthful beauty and sex are synonymous in our culture. Whenever sex is used to sell a product, you can bet that a young and beautiful model is to be found somewhere in the advertisement. If, in fact, these beautiful models are accurately perceived as somewhat "cold" by boyfriends who no longer find static beauty sufficient to arouse desire, then equating model-like beauty with sex is, indeed, ironic. But of course, most male consumers of beautiful women in the media never have to concern themselves with getting used to the same beautiful woman. Men are bombarded with a seemingly endless supply of ever-changing beauties in the media. None of the beautiful women portrayed in the media stay around long enough for the habituation phenomenon to take place.

One can reasonably draw inferences about the inner person based upon what they see on the outside, but the inferences are not always intuitive. Take, for example, the younger woman we see in the grocery store who happens to have had her lips and breasts enlarged, her thighs liposculpted, her hair colored, has a tan and wears a short skirt with 5-inch heels. The inferences that many women make about this person include that she really must think that she is "hot," and that she is flaunting her wares for all to see because she is so taken with herself. The inferences that men make about this same woman is that she is "easy" and that she is hyper-sexual. Both sets of inferences are probably not accurate.

First of all, overt displays of sexuality are seldom what they appear to be. Attention getting reflects an exaggerated *need* to have others look at you. All things being equal, the efforts one makes and the extent to which a person will go to garner attention from others is inversely related to that person's self confidence. Thus, the more outlandish the dress, the more attention-getting cosmetic surgery had, the less the belief in self that without such measures, others will pay attention to you. Using our example from above, we can draw the following inferences about substance based upon looks. First, the woman's need to be looked at is exaggerated. My work has shown that much of the exaggerated need to be looked at derives from a belief, formed in childhood, that the attention garnered came from being pretty, cute and special. Secondly, the woman believes that the only things that will get her the attention she craves are image stimuli. Thus, whether there is a basis for the feeling or not, the woman feels insecure about her inner worth and her value to others when looks are removed from the equation. We also know that she gets a lot of looks, which means that she is probably never satisfied with the amount of attention she gets because she both requires and gets a lot of attention. What this means, for example, is that for an average woman, a look here or a look there is satisfying. To our woman above, 15 looks may be disappointing. We know that she is high-maintenance and self-conscious. We know that she probably will not be sexual with someone who is perceived by her as *only* infatuated with her breasts or some other physical characteristic. But ironically, given the dramatic manner in which this woman presents her physical attributes, it would take a detective to find something other than a physical characteristic to find attractive.

Inner self is affected by external image, and vice versa. One may not be able to judge a book by its cover, but one can always find an inter-relatedness if image and substance are examined closely. Beautiful people are relegated to certain vocations, even when their talents would allow them to pursue many other careers. The invisible barriers set up for beautiful people are everywhere, and not always readily apparent. Sometimes the perks and rewards for pursuing an image-based vocation are too enticing to ignore for a beautiful person. Strippers who can earn 10 times more dancing than they can, for example, teaching, are confronted with a vocational choice which pits their sense of duty to others and, perhaps, their real vocational love, against the freedom and lifestyle which dancing nude can provide. Average-looking people are not confronted with such moral dilemmas in their lives.

Chapter XIII: Beauty and Genetic Engineering

ankind's fascination and obsession with beauty will undoubtedly take on new meaning in the decades ahead. One of the most telling contexts for mankind's future fascination with beauty will be in the field of genetic engineering. Without a doubt, mankind will learn to genetically engineer the beautiful body. Rudimentary gene manipulation has already been achieved. We can splice, cut and replace one gene for another. The vast majority of physical characteristics are controlled by numerous genes working together, that is, they are polygenic in nature. Eye color, on the other hand, is a single pair of genes or an allele. Learn the code, then make the change to the eye color allele, and you will be able to choose the color of your baby's eyes. Will everyone have blue eyes in the future?

In the year 2000, mankind compiled, for the first time, every part of the human DNA blueprint. We may not know, for example, where the nose genes are, but do know that somewhere in our new disorganized compendium those genes exist, awaiting identification and manipulation. As that technology evolves, the ability to identify, remove and replace genes at will is an inevitability.

The reader may find the following facts interesting as it relates to our genetic complement. Keep in mind as I recount some of the more interesting facts that the "wired in" universals of beauty are programmed into our genotype. Also keep in mind that whatever characteristics culture defines as beautiful, such as symmetry or blue eyes, those are also coded on the human genome. Here are some of the more interesting facts: We humans have approximately 25,000 genes, with some estimates as high as 40,000, while others put the number at 21,000 genes. The fruit fly, by comparison, has 13,602 genes. Before the reader feels too special with regard to the size of his genome, some rice plants have over 50,000 genes. Of those genes, which are comprised of letter codes, the individual letters in the human being number approximately three billion. If written out, a human genetic code would require 200 phone-book sized volumes, each consisting of 1000 pages. Speaking of written code, if a person could type 60 words per minute for eight hours a day, it would take 50 years to type out the human genome. If all the DNA in our bodies was put end to end, it would be 600 times greater than the distance to the sun and back again. And speaking of beauty, the DNA of humans is 99.4% IDENTICAL to that of a chimpanzee. So those beautiful blue eyes, blond hair and symmetrical face and lips are located somewhere in that .6% difference between man and the chimpanzee.

Whenever I discuss the topic of genetic engineering and beauty, my audience typically responds with wonderment and speculation about what people will do with a technology which will allow them to manipulate their child's beauty. We already know the answer. We know, because in the future the only thing that is likely to change is the method of change, not what and how we will change it. Notwithstanding a change in mankind's fascination with beauty, man will always strive to be beautiful. Whether accomplished with the scalpel, makeup, designer swimsuit or the genetic engineer, the motivation for change is the same.

One way to predict the future is to closely examine the present. In the early part of the twenty-first century the number of egg transplants, that is, where one woman provides one of her eggs to another woman, was doubling every two years. In the year 1998, there were a little over 7,000 such egg transactions.

With the egg business booming, a cottage industry of "egg brokers" has become a driving force in this version of genetic engineering. Brokers typically receive $3,000 to $5,000 for uniting donor with recipient. A quick perusal of some of the ads placed for donor eggs provides us with insight into what the future will hold.

Here are some representative samples from ads placed in the student newspapers of some of America's finest educational institutions:

1. *"Egg Donor Needed! $15,000.00 and a loving couple seeks a young woman between 18-30 to donate her eggs. Must be: 5'7" - 5' 10" Blonde/Strawberry Blonde/Red Head • Blue or Green Eyes • Slight Build • S.A.T. Scores Starting at 1300 • GPA 3.5 or Higher • Athletic, Outgoing and Beautiful."*

2. *"Give the Gift of Love & Life • Very Special Egg Donor Needed • Our Donor will have the following qualities: Caucasian • Under 30 years old • Athletic for athletic family • Proven college level athletic ability preferred-family waiting. Compensation is $100,000. All expenses will be paid in addition to your compensation paid to you and/or the charity of your choice."*

3. *"EGG DONOR NEEDED • LARGE FINANCIAL INCENTIVE • Intelligent, Athletic Egg Donor Needed For Loving Family • You must be at least 5'10" • Have a 1400+ S.A.T. score • Possess no major family medical issues • $50,000 • Free Medical Screening.*

Ron Harris, a photographer and Arabian horse breeder by profession, shocked the bioethics world when he placed "model's eggs" up for auction in the Fall of 1999. His website at the time: **Ronsangels.com** was asking as much as $150,000 for the eggs of beautiful women. Perhaps even more interesting were some of the comments and criticisms Harris received. For instance, as reported in the L.A. Times in October of 1999, a fertility expert by the name of Bill Handel reportedly said: "If people want to spend $150,000 for the eggs of a gorgeous woman who has an IQ of 68, let them." The assumption that Mr. Handel made about the inverse relationship between beauty and IQ isn't supported in the literature, but is, a classic example of the prejudices beautiful women face. It appears clear that the men and women who are shopping genetic profiles place a great deal of emphasis upon physical attributes, not the least of which is beauty. Attention to beauty isn't always played up in the written solicitations for egg donors, but when the person–to-person interview takes place, beauty becomes a dominant and often deciding factor in the egg donor actually chosen. As far as those attributes openly solicited by egg buyers, height seems to be a premium characteristic, as are high S.A.T. scores. While height may be a genetically defined trait, S.A.T. score performance is at least as much influenced by sociocultural factors as it is genetic programming. Moreover, the irony of these modern eugenicists, who are out shopping for genetically "superior" eggs, is the fact that for whatever reason their personal genetic viability, as measured by the ability to reproduce, is fatally flawed and arguably inferior.

If these ads for donor eggs are any indication, it seems clear that when genetic engineering technology catches up with mankind's obsession with markers of beauty, anyone who is not blond/blue/tall/smart and pretty will be on a genetically dead end street, that is, at least as far as Caucasian "genetic engineers" are concerned.

Assume for a moment that in the future, women will be more beautiful than the average woman today. We can safely assume that a homogenization in looks will occur. Such a homogenization in looks has, in fact, begun with the assistance of makeup and plastic surgery. This homogenization occurs because those involved in the quest for ideal beauty use the same standard of what is considered ideal. For example, the patient who has undergone elective facial aesthetic surgery looks similar to others who have had the same kind of work, for this very reason. What will happen to the quest for beauty? It will continue. The changes which are part and parcel to the quest for beauty will likely become more subtle.

What are the physical traits we value? We value taller, thinner, larger breasts, blue and/or green eyes, blond hair, white teeth, thin waists, broad shoulders, larger genitalia (for men), moderately sized feet, longer fingers and larger eyes, among others.

What should frighten the reader right now is that the eugenics movement of the 1930's in the United States and the Nazis' quest to engineer the ideal race during the 1930's and 1940's valued the exact same traits. With 90 percent of the world made up of people of color, what the bioengineering movement of the future may do is unwittingly engage in a form of genocide against the shorter, brown-eyed, fuller-figured and dark-haired person.

What the reader may find to be of particular interest is that those individuals who possess the "unpopular" physical characteristics, e.g., shorter, darker skinned, etc., share such prejudices, right along with their taller and fairer-skinned brothers and sisters. In the United States, at least, both blacks and whites prefer skin tones which are neither too dark nor too light.

In China, where much of the population is "shorter" compared to European standards, citizens are turning to a risky form of surgery to increase their height. Craig S. Smith, who wrote an article in the Spring of 2002 for the New York Times News Service, noted that "Hundreds of young Chinese, more women than men, obsessed with stature in this increasingly crowded and competitive society, are stretching themselves to new heights on a latter day rack, originally developed by the Russian physician Ilizarov 40 years ago to treat dwarfism and deformed limbs. In addition, the Chinese buy millions upon millions of dollars worth of herbal height enhancers, magnets which promise to stimulate growth hormone and any number of exercises which promise to increase height" Noting the current cultural trends in Bejing, Smith commented: "The Chinese are at least as aware of height as Americans are of hair or skin color. It is one of the first attributes offered or asked about when discussing someone new, particularly a person of the opposite sex. Newspaper classified sections are sprinkled with sought-after heights. Matchmakers and personal advertisements are particularly precise in their prerequisites."

We alter skin tone with both over-the-counter and prescription skin bleach. We buy colored contact lenses (can you guess the color we prefer? Why, blue, of course) and we whiten our teeth. When it comes to altering the color of our teeth, sales of toothpastes with a whitening claim jumped 22 percent, to $570.3 million in the year ended March 23, 2002 (Source: Nielsen scanner data taken from supermarkets, drugstores and mass merchants). Proctor and Gamble introduced a product in 2001 it called "Crest Whitestrips." This home teeth-whitening product costs approximately $44 dollars. P&G estimated that first-year sales from this one product would approach $200 million.

In 2002 the sales of penis "growth" pills were skyrocketing. One manufacturer reported that it sold one million capsules of "penis pills" a month. With each bottle containing 60 pills, a month's supply, that comes out to nearly 17,000 bottles a month. The retail price of those pills is $59.95, which means that this one particular marketer is selling nearly $100,000 a month in "penis pills."

Chapter XIV: Howard Stern

I am sure that many readers will question the logic behind dedicating an entire chapter to Howard Stern in a book about beauty. The explanation for doing so is illustrative of the quest to understand the meanings behind beauty, so let me begin.

Howard Stern is the self-proclaimed "King of All Media," a title that the objective observer is hard-pressed to dismiss, given that he is, and has been for 20 years, the host of a very popular morning radio show, a best-selling author, an actor in a movie about his own life story entitled "Private Parts," and a producer of original television programming, as well as being a television personality at large. When Howard makes a guest appearance on any of the late-night talk shows, the Nielsen ratings predictably skyrocket.

Howard's morning radio program, which originates from New York City and is syndicated across the United States and some parts of Canada, along with being televised on the "E" television network nightly, provides the best opportunity for seasoned listeners and newcomers alike to appreciate the Stern-beauty connection. Longtime listeners of Howard's radio program know that he is obsessed with his own physical appearance as well as the appearance of others.

One of the reasons I have included a chapter under his name is that Howard has, over the years, spoken quite articulately and with great insight about the often subtle and frequently profound impact of physical appearance on virtually every aspect of our culture. His classroom on beauty, also known as his radio show, is often clever, entertaining, brilliant, self-deprecating and, as his critics rail, can be humiliating and cruel.

For those few who are not familiar with the Howard Stern radio program, here is a primer on the show's cast and format. Howard's live radio show is an extension of his personality. He invented a radio format (now so frequently copied that its originator is sometimes forgotten) wherein he and his coterie of friends interact as a family, including the discussion of personal matters, squabbles and familiar banter. Howard introduces into this mix the regular fare of show business guests who stop by to promote their latest project, a few "friends of the show," and Howard's stock in trade, a virtual bevy of strippers, topless dancers, porn stars and an endless stream of girls who audit Professor Stern's class on the importance of physical attractiveness.

Howard's family is made up of Robin Quivers, Gary Dell'Abate, Jackie Martling, Fred Norris, K.C. Armstrong and a few other "cast members." Martling left the show sometime in early 2001 after a long relationship with Howard and the show. He was replaced by Artie Lange, who is now the newest member of Howard's on-air radio family. The extended members of his family include Scott "The Engineer," Ralph Cirella, John "The Stutterer," and his station manager Tom Chiusano. Howard's show is frequented by regulars who make up what he calls the "wack pack." These include "High-Pitch" Eric, "Beetlejuice," Hank "The Angry Dwarf" (now deceased) and others who possess some oddity in personality, and always a peculiar appearance.

Robin Quivers is referred to as "Howard's Nubian princess," a moniker that when fleshed out refers to her pretty face and voluptuous breasts." Gary Dell'Abate, also known as "Ba Ba Booey" or "The Horse Tooth Jackass," is Howard's producer, who has been continually targeted for harassment due, in large measure, to his rather prominent front teeth and lips. Jackie "The Jokeman" Martling was forever being referred to as the "old man." Fred "The Martian" Norris is targeted for his supposed eccentric behavior. K.C.'s sexual preference is a hot topic on the show, while Artie Lange's ample midriff makes him the butt of numerous "fat" jokes.

"Wack pack" member Beetlejuice is a man approximately four feet tall with an odd appearance that is only matched by his attitude. Before his death, Hank "The Angry Dwarf" virtually always appeared under the influence of alcohol. "High Pitch Eric" is an overweight man with, as his nickname suggests, a very high-pitched voice that reminds one of the voice associated with Mickey Mouse. For his part, Howard appears to be dedicated to this eccentric group. A good part of that dedication derives from the fact that these individuals, like Howard himself, felt rejected by beautiful women at one point in their lives. All of that changed once they met Howard Stern, "the king of all media." It is interesting that Howard, the person, could say the same thing.

Howard has spoken at length about his self-judged unattractiveness. "Can you imagine what I had to go through, having to grow up with this face?" Howard often asks of attractive guests of both genders. One gets the sense that Howard never developed the defenses that would have protected him from the reality that people judge other people by how they look. According to Howard, he was continually rejected by girls and women during his formative years, a fact that dominates his reaction to the seemingly endless stream of attractive women who now fawn over "Howard Stern" the media star. Howard is always a hair's breadth away from feeling that all-too-familiar childhood pain at the hands of those prettier than he. Part of his charm and genuineness is that he, unlike others who gained fame and fortune later in life, never lost touch with what it's like to be the odd man out. Howard typically quizzes his attractive female guests about their alleged attraction to him, declaring that he is fully aware that unless he were famous, his beautiful female guests wouldn't give him the time of day.

Howard's ability to articulate the true source of his relatively newfound attraction is an endearing quality, and suggests a sophisticated level of psychological development and/or an inability or refusal to immerse himself in the myth that virtually every other wealthy or famous man engages in. Howard has remained true to the emotions and compatriots of his early developmental years, and can't or won't allow himself to forget what it was like to be rejected because of one's looks. Howard identifies with his "odd" family and even "odder" guests. He has, at one time or another, felt people looked at him the way others look at Beetlejuice and the rest of the "wack pack." He has felt the same anger that plagued Hank "The Angry Dwarf."

Howard has "set up" any number of unattractive men with beautiful women. He has given scores of rejected men the opportunity to be with beautiful women. Howard's fascination with the disabled is more than what his critics would assail as a sadistic pleasure from making fun of those who possess some disability. Rather, Howard has provided a few select downtrodden and rejected men the opportunity to have what men in this society prize the most: a beautiful woman. The women are willing to engage in Howard's beauty-based Marshall plan for the rejected men of the world because Howard allows them to share in his fame.

Howard understands, perhaps better than any other high-profile personality, women who possess fame or fortune based solely upon their beauty. Howard, with uncanny precision, is not shy about reminding beautiful women that it is the "beauty stupid" that accounts for their popularity. Here is a case in point. One repeat guest is a woman named Stacy Rutger. She is an attractive blond with, as Howard describes, a "smokin' little body." Stacy is one of those women who believes that her fame and attention either derives from, or at the very least should derive from, her inner qualities. Other than Howard's show, her only claim to fame is that she appeared in Playboy magazine. The inner quality Stacy wants to be recognized for is her musical talent, something that escapes most listeners, whether they are in the music business or whether they are mere consumers. Despite her desire to be respected for her musical talent, Stacy always shows up for Howard's program dressed in provocative clothing, toting her Playboy layout and latest song: "Give Me More Howard Stern." No matter how persistent Stacy is with the promotion of her singing career, Howard pierces her veil of defenses and reminds her that it is her looks that gets her attention, nothing else. On one show, Stacy appeared with her band members to promote a song which provided Howard with the opportunity to joke with the band members about the reason they work with Stacy.

Howard asked them, in so many words, whether or not it was her musical ability or the fact that she is, to quote Howard, "a hot little piece of ass." Howard had articulated that which remains shrouded in denial in this society. When he does that, he offends sensibilities, but one gets the sense that what is really offensive is that by exposing such hypocrisy, he is denying both the gold-digger and her prey the fantasy that they are together for some, shall we say, more noble reason.

Young, attractive women who exude an arrogance and unapproachableness are one of Howard's favorite targets. One of his favorite techniques is to remind them that the clock is ticking. He muses that virtually all of his female "babe" guests are 25 years old. He reminds them that when their beauty departs, they will be left with nothing but their overwhelmingly boring and grating personality. Each and every time he does this, he gets a little more even for the abject living hell that such women put him through when he still cared.

Howard is a master at piercing the defenses of those who would deny the profound importance of physical attractiveness. Howard is able to strip away the facades, layer by layer, until what is left is the unbridled truth. Case in point: on one show Howard had as his guests three of the contestants from "Who Wants to Marry a Multi-Millionaire?" (See our chapter on *Rich Man/Pretty Woman*). Each of the guests were attractive, and each had participated in the one-time run television program that mated one "lucky lady" from a group of women who competed for the favor of becoming the bride of a multi-millionaire. Virtually every contestant on that show denied that they were trading upon their looks to marry a man with money. During the first 15 minutes of the program, Howard's three guests explicitly denied that looks and money had anything to do with their appearance on that show. Breasts, derrieres, money nor sex itself, had anything to do with what these women were all about, or so they said. This is the kind of denial and hypocrisy that Howard instinctively targets. Piece by piece, Howard moved his guests toward his goal of exposing the truth about their denied agenda of a quid pro quo between beauty and money. After relentlessly stripping away layer after layer of defense, Professor Stern taught a classic lesson. The show ends with two of the women stripping completely naked, for all the world to see, for just a few thousand dollars. Howard had accomplished what no other interviewer could have done.

Howard's skill at talking recalcitrant attractive women out of their clothes for money and gifts is legendary. Attractive women show up to play "Who Wants to be a Turkish Millionaire?" a delightfully funny take-off on ABC's former hit series, "Who Wants to be a Millionaire?" hosted by Regis Philbin. Howard gives away a million Turkish lire, instead of dollars. He delights in stumping beautiful women on seemingly easy questions, often commenting that "You see, they don't have to know anything, they get by with their looks." After they lose, however, at winning the money by failing to recall fourth grade social studies questions, Howard approaches the unsuspecting contestant with various incentives, if they would only show off some part of their body. He often is confronted with protestations and outrage from the contestant—how dare he think that her body could be bought for any price! But Howard, working like a man who instinctually knows the connection, often reminds his beautiful guests that she will not always be beautiful and that her beauty can be translated into material goods if she were to just play along. Like time-lapse photography of the transition through all four seasons, Howard eventually makes the connection and is rewarded with the spectacle of breasts, and sometimes derrieres, for the price of a wristwatch or trip to Mazatlan.

Professor Stern has conducted experiments, with the aid of a hypnotist, in order to achieve for himself and his friends that which was denied him as a younger man. In one particular program, Howard had a hypnotist place three beautiful topless dancers from Scores, a gentleman's club in New York City, under his hypnotic spell. Howard directed that each subject be given a number of post-hypnotic suggestions, including one where the strippers would find him physically irresistible when he activated an electronic buzzer. Howard's legendary feelings of sexual inadequacy could magically be transformed into sexual prowess with one touch of a button.

Each time Howard pushed the button the girls, one by one, experienced the sensations traditionally associated with an orgasm. Howard's pleasure was short lived, however, as reflected in the fact that even during his glee over his hypnotically induced sexual prowess and attraction, he bemoaned that this magical experience was just that, an illusion that only reminded him even more clearly of his deep feelings about his own physical unattractiveness and inadequacy.

Howard incorporated into the same show a member of his wack pak, "Elephant Boy," a hearing-impaired gentleman with a speech impediment who, before Howard, had lived a life of rejection at the hands of women. Howard asked for a post-hypnotic suggestion that would make the strippers find Elephant Boy irresistible. And irresistible he became.

But something occurred when the girls fawned over Elephant Boy, and Howard took note. Elephant Boy treated the strippers' hypnotically induced attraction to him as less related to the power of suggestion and more related to his own newfound attractiveness. Once Howard picked up the defenses of Elephant Boy at work, he immediately had the girls' post-hypnotic suggestion negated and watched with glee as Elephant Boy grappled with the fact that the stripper, who had just moments ago found him irresistible, pulled away from him as though she found him repulsive.

Howard almost always begins each interview of beautiful porn stars with the question: "Were you molested as a child?" He thinks out loud as he delves into the seemingly counterintuitive connection between working as a porn star and being stunningly beautiful. What Howard discovers is that porn stars are often beautiful, but they are virtually always from working class backgrounds and lack the imagination required to parlay their looks into some other more socially acceptable profession that would pay as well. Indeed, the demand for beauty is high, but the supply of women willing to do almost anything in trade for their beauty is higher. Those beautiful women who do make it in modeling or acting are a rarity. Try and name 20 living, famous beautiful women and you will see how rare it really is for beautiful women to make it into our consciousness as unique individuals. On the other hand, beautiful women are everywhere, or so it seems, with each one vying for a spot in the Top 20 list.

Howard's affection for porn stars extends well beyond his own personal attraction and the fact that sex sells. One gets the sense that Howard likes their honesty, in that these beautiful women have made the connection between their looks and money, unencumbered by the defenses that often accompany other beautiful women. Howard's unstated thesis is that whether you sleep with an older executive who, in the absence of his wealth, would never garner a second look; bounce around the television set in your bikini believing that you are a serious actress; traipse around the office in a mini-skirt in hopes of gaining the attention of one of the partners in the law firm; or perform sex on camera, it is all the same thing, but for a few minor details. That is one of Howard

Stern's lessons that he so desperately wants to share with us.

Other lessons include the recognition of the pain that unattractive men must endure in our society at the hands of attractive women. Howard wants the lesson learned by all the young, arrogant and unapproachable girls that beauty is inextricably linked to the clock, and that the clock is ticking.

Howard's radio family has learned the lessons that he has chosen to teach in the classroom that his radio show has become. On one occasion, two attractive women in their early twenties made their way into the classroom. Getting their way and gaining access to places that are off-limits to less attractive women had become a way of life for them. On this particular day in class, the game centered around the value that Howard and his staff placed on their beauty and the value the guests placed upon their beauty. Howard wanted a trade: show your breasts and you get to be on the show. It was clear that these women had honed the tease game with precision. It was clear that they had never before been denied anything by men, at least until today. Once the girls arrived in the green room, they informed Howard's producer, Gary Dell'Abate, that they had decided to renege on their promise to show their breasts. It was clear that they believed that their mere presence and beauty would be enough to get them air time. Gary looked at the women and said words to the effect: "Look, you may be the hottest chicks in your home town, but you're just another day at work for us. Either take off your tops or leave. Gary told them that tomorrow, 20 more beautiful women will be trying to get on the show, and that now is the time to show or go. The look on the women's faces bore an uncanny resemblance to the look on the faces of thousands of pretty girls across the world who come to Hollywood each year to become famous. Those girls may have been considered the most beautiful in their home town, but Hollywood is the big league, and although it seems impossible, the supply of women trying to make money because of their looks actually outstrips demand.

Howard's critics almost always focus upon his cruel and sometimes unforgiving criticisms of others. Howard's criticisms almost always focus on some element of his target's looks, but the motive to engage in such criticism almost always stems from Howard's assessment of his target's disingenuousness and/or hypocrisy. It seems clear, however, that the depth and intensity with which Howard does almost anything has been inexorably imprinted by his relationship to, and feelings about, beauty. (SEE PHOTO CREDITS OF HOWARD STERN)

Howard Stern Pictured at Various Stages in His Life

Chapter XV: September 11, 2001

On September 11, 2001, the world changed forever. What followed the September 11 attacks was a crash course in Islamic fundamentalism, especially as practiced by the millions of devotees of Osama bin Laden. The steep learning curve of that crash course was focused upon trying to understand the hatred that millions upon millions of Muslim fundamentalists have for America. I should note at this point that in classical Arabic, no word exists for "fundamentalism." Arabic linguists have, therefore, coined the term "usuliyya," which means "basic principles." It is a term, rightly or wrongly, that has come to refer to what Westerners understand as a fundamentalist interpretation of Islam.

One element of the hatred Islamic fundamentalists have for the Western world has not received its due attention. This inattention is remarkable, because this one element permeates their attitudes about America. This one element affects virtually everything fundamentalists believe, and everything they do and practice. It is a constant modifier of not only the fundamentalist's daily lives, but one of the most articulated aspects of their hatred for America. It defines, on a daily basis, their very consciousness.

The perpetrators of the events on September 11 had and have very strong beliefs when it comes to the subject of feminine beauty. In fact, much of their hatred of Western culture is intertwined with their hatred of Western culture's emphasis upon beauty, with a particular focus upon the display of feminine beauty.

Tahera Aftab, an expert on both the subject of Islam and women, is a professor at Gettysburg College, located in Pennsylvania. According to Aftab, Islam requires women not to attract men, and specifically not to show their hair or their beauty. The Koran does not, however, specifically demand that women cover their face. It follows quite logically, however, that the more conservative, or fundamentalist, if you will, the particular political order which accedes power to its Muslim religious leaders, the more repressive will be the restrictions upon women's expression of their beauty. Whether it is the "Nikab" in Pakistan, the "Chador" in Iran, or the full body and face covering called the "Burka" in Afghanistan, the purpose is always the same. Muslim women's wear is singularly designed to suppress physical attractiveness, a purpose which is exactly the opposite in the West.

The dichotomy between the West and the Muslim world is never clearer than when considering women's dress and the motivations which define its style. After the events of September 11, the *Seattle Times* provided its readers with a primer on Muslim dress for women. The beautifully executed illustrations which accompanied that article, drawn by Paul Schmid, are included herein. (SEE PHOTO CREDITS OF MUSLIM CLOTHING FROM AROUND THE WORLD).

Millions of Muslim men find Western women to be nothing more than cheap whores, a conclusion based in large measure upon how Western women display their beauty. It is nearly impossible to overstate the depth of hated felt by fundamentalist Muslims when it comes to Western expressions of beauty. The hatred to which I make reference is visceral in nature. It extends deeper than all of the well-known intellectual arguments utilized by some of the pundits in the West to rationalize the Muslim fundamentalist's hostility toward the United States, e.g., Palestinian-Israeli issue, "infidels" in the holy and, jealousy of the West, etc. It is as though the lyrics of ths song of hatred are made up of political issues, while the music and beat are wholly derived from the fundamentalist's feelings about sexuality and the expressions of feminine beauty.

To illustrate how the events of September 11 are inextricably linked to beauty, one need only reference the teachings of none other than Osama bin Laden. In an infamous terrorist training video, first seen after the attacks on the World Trade Center and the Pentagon, bin Laden decried the fact that Saudi Arabia had been infiltrated with Jews and Christians. Osama bin Laden delivered this part of his speech with quiet solemnity. His objections are based upon the fact that Mecca, located in Saudi Arabia, is the most holy of all places on earth, from the Muslim perspective. But bin Laden's quiet rationalizations and controlled demeanor about the "infidels" who occupy the holy land pale when he begins to talk about the specifics. He becomes quite emotional and agitated when he declares that not only are there "infidels" in Saudi Arabia, but even female Jews and Christians are in the holy land. His anger and emotional fervor, as seen on the tape, crescendo when he reaches the climactic point of his story. Not only are there female Jews and Christians in Saudi Arabia, he states, but worst of all, *pretty* female Jews and Christians occupy the holy land.

One of the leaders of the attacks on the World Trade Center, a man by the name of Mohammed Atta, had with him a note which kept his mind focused on the task at hand. That note included any number of references to how he should look and dress. For example, under point number one, Atta is reminded of how he needs to look for the afterlife:

1. Pledge allegiance to die, and the renewal of steps to be alert.
 * shaving of extra body hair, wearing fragrance. * wash up.

Under heading number 14, Atta was reminded of how he should dress:

14. Wear your cloth appropriately — tied, the way our good ancestors did it, may God bless them, they used to wear their cloth in a tied fashion.

On page three of Atta's list he is reminded of the *beautiful* angels that await him after he

Moroccan Nikab

Illustrations by Paul Schmid of the *Seattle Times*
Narrative Descriptions by the *Seattle Times*

The nikab is the form of Muslim veiling that comes
closest to what is actually meant by the English word
"veil." English speakers tend to use the word veil as a
catch-all term that covers all types of Muslim head and
body coverings. The nikab, worn in black by this
Moroccan woman, is a veil in the true sense of the word.
It covers everything below the bridge of the nose and the
upper cheeks, and sometimes also covers the forehead.

Pakistani Nikab

Illustrations by Paul Schmid of the *Seattle Times*
Narrative Descriptions by the *Seattle Times*

Many Pakistani Muslims, such as this one, wear some form of veil.
This woman is wearing the nikab along with a bandana that reads,
"God is great!" The veil existed before Islam existed, but it has been
embraced and spread by the religion. Not all Muslim women wear a veil,
but among those who do, styles vary wildly, from simple kerchiefs and
elaborate head scarves to full face-and-body coverings.

Dupatta

Illustrations by Paul Schmid of the *Seattle Times*
Narrative Descriptions by the *Seattle Times*

Hindu women also wear a veil, a practice that highlights
the fact that veiling is not exclusively Muslim. Traditional
and orthodox Hindu women, such as this one, will cover
their heads and at least partly obscure their faces in the
company of unrelated adult males. Sometimes veiling is
accomplished with a loose end of the woman's sari, and
sometimes it is done with a scarf-like fabric known as the
dupatta.

Chador

Illustrations by Paul Schmid of the *Seattle Times*
Narrative Descriptions by the *Seattle Times*

The chador is the full-body cloak Muslim women in
Iran are expected to wear outdoors. Depending on
how it is designed and on how the woman holds it,
the chador may or may not cover the face. The chador
was forbidden in Iran under the reign of Mohammad
Reza Shah, who was brought to power with help from
the United States and sought to modernize the country.
After the shah was exiled during the Islamic
Revolution in 1979, the chador became required wear
for all Iranian women. Many Iranians today subvert
their dress-code by wearing Western-style clothing
beneath the chador.

Hijab

Illustrations by Paul Schmid of the *Seattle Times*
Narrative Descriptions by the *Seattle Times*

The word hijab refers to the variety of styles in
which Muslim women use scarves and large pieces
of cloth to cover their hair, neck and sometimes
shoulders. As shown on this Seattle-area Muslim
woman, the hijab often leaves the entire face open. In
the United States, the hijab is the most common form
of headcovering for Muslim women.

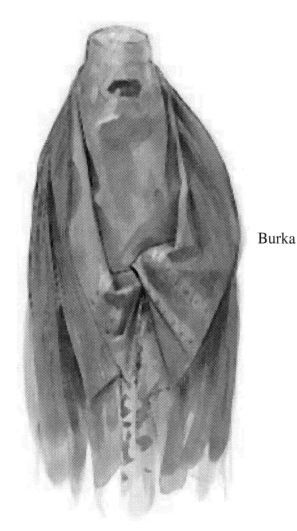

Burka

Illustrations by Paul Schmid of the *Seattle Times*
Narrative Descriptions by the *Seattle Times*

The burka comes in many variations, but in its most
conservative form, it thoroughly covers the face of the
person wearing it, leaving only a mesh-like screen to see
through. This refugee is wearing the conservative burka
that the Taliban regime requires women in Afghanistan to
don outdoors. The burka is thought to have originated in
the Arabian peninsula and can still be found there today.
They are not always as conservative in form as the one
shown here and often allow parts of a woman's face to
show through.

crashes his plane into its target: *Also do not appear to be nervous, be happy with a happy heart, be confident because you are doing a job that religion accepts and loves. And then there will be a day that you will spend with beautiful angels [hur 'een] in Paradise. Oh young Man keep a smiling face. You are on your way to everlasting Paradise.* (Source: ABC News translation of Atta's note, originally written in Arabic).

Salmon Rusdie has argued that the Muslim world's fear of Westernization is at the heart of its hatred for America. He wrote the following in a widely disseminated editorial two months after the World Trade Center and Pentagon attacks: "For a vast number of "believing" Muslim men, "Islam" stands, in a jumbled, half-examined way, not only for the fear of God—the fear more than the love, one suspects—but also for a cluster of customs, opinions and prejudices that include their dietary practices; the sequestration or near sequestration of "their" women; the sermons delivered by their mullahs of choice; a loathing of modern society in general, riddled as it is with music, godlessness and sex; and a more particularized loathing (and fear) of the prospect that their own immediate surrounding could be taken over—"Westoxicated"—by the liberal Western-style way of life." That liberal Western-style way of life is virtually defined by the West's obsessive fascination with the expression of feminine beauty and the sexuality it intends to project. Images coming from the West of teen girls dressed in mini skirts, reports of overt expressions of sexuality in middle school, music videos, film and television shows which include nudity or seductive clothing, are perceived as a direct threat to Islamic principles of morality, in addition to representing a primal and powerful threat to the emotional security of husbands, fathers and boyfriends. One cannot underestimate the power and influence of such primal threats to male emotional security.

The crash course on Muslim fundamentalism after September 11 included the topic of martyrdom. It was, after all, martyrs who gave their lives willingly in the attacks. What we learned is that sexuality is at the heart of the promised land awaiting the Muslim who gives his life in service to the eradication of the "infidels." For example, in return for martyrdom, Hamas tells its students that their families will be financially compensated, their pictures will be posted in schools and mosques, and they will earn a special place in heaven. They also are promised unlimited sex with 72 virgins in heaven. In one of the passages of the Koran, it is said the martyrs and virgins shall "delight themselves, lying on green cushions and beautiful carpets." The Koran extols the beauty of the virgins who await the martyr.

The Koran describes the virgins as "beautiful like rubies, with complexions like diamonds and pearls." This passage in the Koran suggests that the Western "infidels" and their Muslim counterparts may not be all that different in their definitions of beauty. Just consider that one of the motivators for martyrdom, made mention of in the Koran, is the beautiful complexion of the virgins who await the martyr. Dermatologists in both the West and the Muslim world strive to give their patients complexions like diamonds and pearls while still living in this life.

Jack Kelly, a reporter for USA Today, visited Hamas-run kindergartens, where he noted signs on the walls which read: "The children of the kindergarten are the shaheeds (holy martyrs) of tomorrow." Kelly noted that the classroom signs at Al-Najah University in the West Bank and at Gaza's Islamic University read, "Israel has nuclear bombs, we have human bombs." Kelly made special note of an 11-year-old Palestinian student named Ahmed. He attended an Islamic school in Gaza City run by Hamas. "I will make my body a bomb that will blast the flesh of Zionists, the sons of pigs and monkeys," Ahmed said. "I will tear their bodies into little pieces and cause them more pain than they will ever know." "Allah Akbar," his classmates shouted in response: "God is great." "May the virgins give you pleasure," his teacher yelled, referring to the beautiful women awaiting martyrs in paradise.

Americans find much of the terrorist's behavior to be hypocritical, to say the least. On the one hand, men force upon "their" women a strict behavioral code which mandates harsh punishments for women who would dare to enhance and display their beauty. (SEE PHOTO CREDITS OF TALIBAN MEN BEATING UNIDENTIFIED WOMAN) At the same time, some of the terrorists who participated in the September 11 attacks on the World Trade Center and the Pentagon frequented nude bars and were regular customers of prostitutes, all of whom painted their nails, wore lots and lots of makeup and exposed their bodies for all to see. In San Diego, where some of the terrorists lived before the attacks, local topless dancers immediately identified their regular terrorist customers from published photographs after the attacks.

When examined closely, we learn how Islamic fundamentalists resolve this apparent hypocrisy. Unless a woman follows the strict behavioral codes set forth by conservative mullahs, she is no longer a woman, but has transformed herself into nothing more than an "infidel," something less than human. It follows, using this logic, that Muslim men are free, therefore, to not treat these "infidel" creatures with the "respect" that burqa-draped women deserve.

But how do these particular men rationalize engaging in the most unholy of Western behaviors, including paying for sex, going to nude bars and drinking alcohol? What the Western world does not realize is that unless you are a true believer, none of the rules apply to not only the "infidel" herself, but those who would interact with her. Hunters use the same logic when killing animals for sport. The hunter would never kill a human being, but because he believes that animals are less than human, not only do they not deserve respect, but the hunter is free to express his most violent of desires, even including killing and abusing non-humans for fun and sport. Many in the Western world do not make such compartmentalized distinctions; and therefore, they are not provided an easy rationalization for behavior that would otherwise be unacceptable.

Muslim men and women can be very passionate. The intense feelings that accompany sexuality are often overwhelming, just as they are for many in the West. In a society where sexual feelings come attached with tremendous strictures, strictures that if violated may even result in death, one can begin to understand how anything that would arouse sexual feelings, especially beauty, would come to be viewed with the greatest of trepidation. Beauty and its various expressions are the primary and dominant way by which sexuality is expressed. Thus, beautiful fingernails, hair, and the female figure hints at sexuality both in America and the Muslim world. In 1990 a "fatwa," or religious ruling, was issued by 200 Afghan mullahs from Peshawar, Pakistan. That document measured 2 by 3 feet. In that particular "fatwa" it was decried that girls should not attend schools or become educated. A year earlier, yet another "fatwa" forbade that women "walk with pride" or walk in the middle of the street. In America, men have learned to enjoy feminine beauty as expressed in walk and dress. "Girl watching" is a national pastime in America; it is a punishable offense in many fundamentalist Muslim countries.

In some sense, beauty and its various expressions are given even greater value in the fundamentalist Muslim world, compared to America. Virginity is tantamount to sexual attraction to many Muslims. In America, elective virginity is reflective of an adherence to a moral code which may or may not be equated with sexual attraction. American men have learned to control themselves when confronted with women who purposely engage in every imaginable technique designed to increase their beauty. Once afflicted with attraction to beauty, a fundamentalist Muslim is forced to transform, then project onto the woman who attracted him, his own love/hate reaction to beauty. Thus, the woman who displays beauty is subliminally loved while consciously hated.

Displays of beauty can function as a lighting rod for fundamentalist Muslims. In late November of 2002, over 100 people were killed and over 500 injured in riots in Nigeria, a country which is approximately half Muslim and half Christian. The riots culminated months of protest and unrest by fundamentalist Muslims over the 2002 Miss World Beauty Pageant which was to be held in Nigeria. The riots occurred when the daily newspaper in Lagos, Nigeria, "This Day," published an article which proffered the idea that none other than the prophet Mohammed, himself, would probably have chosen a wife from among the Miss World contestants. (SEE PHOTO CREDIT OF MISS WORLD CONTESTANTS IN NIGERIA)

Even before the riots, fundamentalist Islamic clerics declared a serious religious emergency the result of Nigeria's playing host to the Miss World Beauty Pageant. Nigeria's Muslim fundamentalists have strong feelings when it comes to women's sexual behavior. In fact, several women have been sentenced to death by stoning for conceiving children out of wedlock, behavior that provides incontrovertible evidence of what can happen to women who are, by definition, sexually attractive to men.

Once again, we confirm that beauty is a double-edged sword, whether you live in America or a fundamentalist Muslim country. Beauty is to be shackled in this world by fundamentalist Muslims, while at the same time functioning in the afterlife world as the ultimate reward for those Muslims who would die as martyrs.

(*Left and Below*)
Taliban Male Beating
a Woman

AP Photo

Miss World Contestants Protected by Armed Guard in Nigeria

The repression of beauty remains fixed in the presence of other advances toward equality between the sexes. Thus, the fundamentalist has less of a problem with women who are empowered politically and economically, than he does with their expressions of feminine beauty through clothing, makeup and body language. Turkey, Pakistan, Indonesia and Bangladesh, all Muslim-dominated countries, have had female prime ministers, while maintaining strict behavioral codes which regulate the expression of feminine beauty. The same is true for Egypt, which provides its working women with any number of employment protections, including child-care leave and maternity leave. Still, the most revolutionary thing that a woman can do, in most Muslim countries, is to reveal or enhance her beauty.

On November 20, 2001, several hundred Afghan women demonstrated in the streets of Kabul, Afghanistan. The most revolutionary acts that these women engaged in during their demonstration, the behaviors that got most of the attention, involved such things as daring to wear sandals and lifting their burqas to show their faces. Even when the schools for women re-open, the beatings stop and women again are allowed to gain a political equal footing with men, the strictures on the expressions of their beauty shall, in all likelihood, remain.

Los Angeles Times writer David Lamb has noted that a year after the September 11 attacks, women all across the Arab world, women of all classes, are "putting on the hijab, the head scarf their grandmothers fought to take off a half a century ago as the symbol of women's oppression." This conservative trend is something that has surprised many Westerners, who believed that once Afghanistan was rid of the Taliban, and once America embarked upon its war on terror, a move toward Western values would soon follow. Mr. Lamb quoted Omniya Mahmoud, a 27-year-old teacher who lives in Cairo and who began wearing a veil for the first time after the attacks on America: "I used to be the type who really took care of what I wore, dyed my hair, put on makeup, but when I started the (religion) classes, I found lots of other women my age. I realized this was the right thing to do. It is what God wants."

Chapter XVI: Scientific Research

This chapter is designed for the reader who may wish to learn about some of the latest and most interesting scientific research on the subject of beauty. *Awakening Beauty* is rooted in scientific research. I chose, however, to not overly burden the reader with research citation after citation in the body of this work because I wanted to create a book that was fun and easy to read for everyone. Having expressed that thought, however, for those readers who may be interested in a brief overview of recent scientific research on beauty, I offer this chapter. As the reader will discover, many of the researchers who study physical attractiveness are thoughtful and incorporate clever methodologies in their studies that often yield very interesting findings.

The Pitfalls of "Thin"

An interesting study from England has put forth a very provocative explanation for the epidemic of eating disorders among young women in Western countries. This study confirmed one of the primary tenets of our chapter on *The Cult of the Beautiful Egg,* by documenting the virulent effect of sexual competition among women in a society which focuses upon culturally defined standards of beauty, in this instance, being thin. The researcher documented the proposition, to quote from the article: "The present-day environment of Western countries presents a range of conditions which have led to the overactivation or the disruption of the archaic female sexual strategy of maximizing mate value."

When "thin" is synonymous with being sexually desirable, while at the same time Nature herself is forever laying down fat deposits, it is no wonder that some women who are competing for such desirability will stop at nothing in order to "win." Men add to this female-female competitive frenzy by demanding unrealistic body shapes and sizes from their ideal mates. But what happens when you achieve the moniker of beautiful from others? Do you become less competitive and concerned about such things as weight?

By way of introduction to the next study, numerous researchers have looked at the relationship between one's own subjective sense of physical attractiveness and being concerned about one's weight and diet. Those studies seem to show that the prettier you subjectively feel, the less likely you are to be overly concerned about your weight and diet. As the next study informs us, however, the issue is not so simple nor is it straightforward.

In a study which documented one of the many liabilities associated with being beautiful, researchers from York University in Canada found that being objectively judged to be physically beautiful placed one at risk for developing an eating disorder. Importantly, these researchers removed the variables of body size and neurotic perfectionism as an explanation for their results. Consider what may be at work here. Once a woman achieves beauty, the pressure to maintain that level of beauty in the eyes of others is tremendous. Adding to the complexities involved here is the fact that one's subjective sense of beauty is inextricably linked to the treatment you receive from others. Since we know women are competitive with one another when it comes to beauty, it may be hard to consistently feel attractive when a woman is an active participant in the beauty marketplace. Moreover, since people tend to put on weight as they age, with every tick of the clock the beautiful woman finds herself looking down the barrel of the loss of her beauty.

First Dates

The world can be unrelenting and extremely harsh for women, when it comes to being evaluated on the dimension of physical attractiveness. This conclusion was recently documented in a study which looked at the quality of a six-minute initial meeting between members of the opposite sex. The researchers wanted, in part, to determine the relative importance men and women give to looks as a factor which predicts the quality of an initial meeting. Not only did a woman's attractiveness rating predict how her male partner would rate the quality of their meeting, with prettier women getting the higher scores, but the researchers found that the women themselves, along with objective observers who watched the six-minute meeting, judged the quality of the interaction between man and woman to be of a higher quality when the woman was prettier. Just as interesting were the findings related to how a man's level of physical attractiveness affected his, the woman's and the objective observer's judgment of the quality of the meeting.

In a finding from this study which documents the unique pressure that women feel, when it comes to looks, the physical attractiveness of the man had nothing to do with the ratings he, the woman or the objective observer gave to the quality of the meeting. For men, the one personality factor which best predicted the quality ratings of the meeting was the man's level of extroversion, with the more extroverted men earning the higher scores. The dynamics at work here illustrate that many women's obsession with their looks does have a basis in reality. What it also means is that men may be defining the quality of first dates by devaluing women's personality in favor of their physical attractiveness. According to this study, if a woman out on a first date feels like an object, it may be because that is exactly what she is.

Crime

An important study for victims of violent crimes illustrated just how important a victim's attractiveness can have on perceptions of the specific type of crime committed against her. To quote from the research paper: "Subjects in two studies were shown portraits of 32 young women who varied widely in physical attractiveness. Subjects were told that half of these women had been victims of a crime, and half had not. Their job was to sort the portraits correctly into those two categories. In both studies, attractive women were more often categorized as victims of rape. In Study 2, attractive women were not more likely to be categorized as having been beaten and robbed. Correlation analyses showed that the association between physical attractiveness and presumed criminal victimization was significantly higher for rape than for being beaten and robbed."

One is left to contemplate the sexual associations made to beautiful women, even if those sexual associations involve criminal conduct. But perhaps a more sinister inference can be drawn from these data if they are viewed from the perspective of the relatively unattractive woman who has been the victim of rape. It may be that an unattractive woman, who has been a victim of rape, would be less likely to be believed in a criminal trial if the evidence were less than conclusive, despite the fact that the crime had actually been committed.

Beauty Cues

Both sexes seem to be utilizing facial cues as indicators of sexual mating choice. It has long been accepted that facial symmetry increases attractiveness for both sexes. And while that is true, the story is much more complex. Researchers from the University of California, at Davis, found that other factors, as well, seem to function as cues about with whom women would like to mate. To quote from the study, "Using photographs of men's faces, for which facial symmetry had been measured, we found a relationship between women's attractiveness ratings of these faces and symmetry, but the subjects could not *consciously* rate facial symmetry accurately. Moreover, the relationship between facial attractiveness and symmetry was still observed, even when symmetry cues were removed by presenting only the left or right half of faces. These results suggest that attractive features other than symmetry can be used to assess phenotypic condition. We identified one such cue, facial masculinity (cheek-bone prominence and a relatively longer lower face), which was related to both symmetry and full and half-face attractiveness."

As previously touched upon, one of the more fascinating aspects of this study is that women's attraction to men could be predicted by assessing a man's facial symmetry, but that women were unable to consciously assess, with any degree of accuracy, the actual symmetry of a man's face. The author's suggest that what women are selecting, when they select a particular facial type, are good genes to mate with. On the other hand, all things being equal, unlike for men when they select women, women are more interested in status and personality than any marker of physical beauty.

A study from Syracuse University supported predictions about mating choice derived from evolutionary theory: Men's assessments of sexual attractiveness are determined more by objectively assessable physical attributes; women's assessments are more influenced by perceived ability and willingness to invest (e.g., partners' social status, potential interest in them). Consequently, women's assessments of potential partners' sexual attractiveness and coital acceptability vary more than men's assessments. One fascinating part of this study involved the investigation of the importance that male beauty had for women who were polygamous. One might think that if women are "playing the field" and not interested in such things as willingness to invest, social status, potential interest in them, commitment, etc., then these women might emphasize a man's looks, not unlike men's attitudes toward women. The researchers found that what women ultimately value in a man was not affected by the fact that they were polygamous. Thus, social status and willingness to invest seem to attract even women who play the field. Men understand and sometimes play upon women's attraction to such behaviors as interest, commitment and willingness to invest. Is it no wonder, then, that an attractive man who divests himself from his commitment and relationship with a woman, suffers her emotional wrath. "Hell hath not fury like a woman scorned," aptly describes any number of the women we have come to know in the media who, at one time, had a relationship with an attractive man, but who later were abandoned by him. In virtually each and every case of these high profile breakups, problems did not arise until the man divested himself from his commitment and interest in the woman who has just become his most vocal critic.

Australian researchers have documented the importance of symmetry in determining what is and what is not beautiful. To quote from their research: "Symmetry is a major correlate of physical attractiveness across species, including humans." The authors of this study went on to acknowledge that investigating the nature of the relationship between beauty and symmetry has been difficult, however, for several reasons, including the facts that variance in symmetry is attributable to more than one source and is often correlated with other variables related to attractiveness.

What the Australian researchers did, in order to neutralize some of the other confounding factors in assessing the importance of symmetry in the assessment of beauty, was to study identical twins who, obviously, look alike. The researchers found: "The more symmetric twin of a pair was consistently rated as more attractive, and the magnitude of the difference between twins in perceived attractiveness was directly related to the magnitude of the difference in symmetry."

In my own experience involving twins, I have found that there exists the colloquial notion that when it comes to female identical twins, one is always considered to be the "prettier" twin. Since identical twins share the exact same genetic blueprint, but differ in both their intra-utero and social environments, anything that may negatively affect symmetry affects the perception of beauty. This study, along with others which have documented mankind's association between beauty and balance, informs us why makeup tricks which balance out a person's face really do make a person more beautiful on a primitive and unconscious level.

Before the reader concludes that the assessment of facial attractiveness is a rather straightforward and simple matter of judging symmetry, I offer the following research findings from the Perception Laboratory at the School of Psychology, University of St. Andrews, United Kingdom.

Through very clever manipulation of visual images, researchers at the lab found that the left side of the human face appears to be more important than the right side, when it comes to judging levels of facial attractiveness. "Following previous studies, we found that subjects' judgments of gender and expression were influenced more by the left than the right side of the face (viewer's perspective). This left of face (viewer's perspective) stimulus bias extended to judgments about facial attractiveness and facial age." When I discussed this work with Dave Perret, one of the authors of this clever study, he told me that "observers are looking in exactly the WRONG place. They should be looking at the right side of the face (viewer's perspective) which corresponds to the observed person's left side. This side (right, from the viewer's perspective) is most likely to show spontaneous unilateral expressions, and hence be a truer reflection of someone's personality." The reasons for the richness of information coming from the right side of the face are rooted in neurophysiology, and are beyond the scope of this book. This study confirms the rich complexities which are part and parcel to any analysis of what makes us beautiful.

When it comes to the overall body type that women find attractive in members of the opposite sex, researchers at Montana State University found that while women preferred a man who possessed, and I quote: "lean/broad-shouldered and average/balanced male types," men emphasized the muscular bulk male type. One has to ask the question: Do male body builders strive to please women or men? If it is women they are trying to impress, they are way off the mark when they strive to achieve muscular bulk, as opposed to a more lean and balanced, broad-shouldered proportionate body type.

For years, researchers have attempted to identify what physical attributes men utilize to evaluate with whom they would like to have sex. According to researchers in England, "Evolutionary psychology suggests that a woman's sexual attractiveness is based on cues of health and reproductive potential." The authors of this study wrote that "In recent years, research has focused on the ratio of the width of the waist to the width of the hips (the waist-to-hip ratio [WHR]). A low WHR (a curvaceous body) is believed to correspond to the optimal fat distribution for high fertility, and so this shape should be highly attractive. "In this paper we present evidence that weight scaled for height (the body mass index [BMI]) is the primary determinant of sexual attractiveness, rather than WHR. BMI is also strongly linked to health and reproductive potential. Furthermore, we show how covariation of apparent BMI and WHR in previous studies led to the overestimation of the importance of WHR in the perception of female attractiveness. Finally, we show how visual cues, such as the perimeter-area ratio (PAR), can provide an accurate and reliable index of an individual's BMI and could be used by an observer to differentiate between potential partners."

One must always temper these results with the stark reality that desiring to have sex with someone is quite different than choosing to exclusively commit to that person. This entire research area of what is biologically sexually attractive is confounded by the widespread use of contraceptives and the fact that women are putting off marriage and waiting to have children until well into their third decade of life. By the time a woman reaches her third decade of life, WHR, BMI and PAR indices have changed from those of the nubile 18- to 25-year-old. Despite the fact that women's bodies change away from sexually attractive indices, what men prefer to have sex with does not.

One of the assumptions of the strictly sociobiological perspective is that when men cue into "fertile" WHR, BMI and PAR indices, they are making a wise reproductive choice. In other words, men's attraction to curvaceous bodies makes biological sense. What men are really cueing into is more related to the fertility of the younger woman, not the overall desirability of a mate to share one's life with. Study after study confirm men's obsession with nubility as a trait that arouses their sexual interest. That sexual interest, however, frequently does not result in commitment to that same curvaceous woman. Consider the harsh conclusion that one beautiful beauty pageant contestant shared with me. She told me that the one thing she has learned, after 10 years of achieving the perfect body, is that when she achieved the "to-die-for curvaceous figure," all she had really gained was that now even more men wanted to have sex with her, not have a meaningful relationship.

If researchers are postulating that a woman's WHR is a "wired-in" characteristic that affects their sexual attractiveness, then what effect does culture have? In a 1993 study conducted at the University of Texas, researchers found that cultural norms do influence, albeit in a minor way, the beauty/WHR connection. Researchers found that minor changes in the WHR's of Miss America winners and Playboy playmates have occurred over the past 30 to 60 years. Those changes reflect the transition from the more full-figured woman to the thinner ideal. By the way, the ideal waist to hip ratio finds the waist approximately 70% of the hip's size.

With reference to modern depictions of beauty, perhaps none is more illustrative of the subtle effects of the determinants of beauty than the Barbie doll. If one looks closely at Barbie, she has an exaggerated WHR; that is, Barbie is significantly more curvaceous than 99 percent of all women. Her breasts are unusually large when compared to her other body proportions. Her derriere, thighs and facial features are exaggerated caricatures of classic beauty. To quote from a study conducted at Fairmont State College in West Virginia: "The long-term acceptance and success of the Barbie doll suggests the physical characteristics of the doll are perceived as attractive." When viewed in the context of universal attractiveness, response to the doll raises the question of why Barbie is perceived as attractive. Published paleontological data on hominid fossils indicate how the shapes and anatomical proportions of humans have evolved. Included in the fossils are phenotypic traits no longer prevalent in humans (primitive) and phenotypic traits that have become increasingly prevalent (derived). It is noted that the anatomical proportions of the Barbie doll are exaggerated and emphasize derived characteristics. It was proposed that in the perception of human form, derived traits are perceived as attractive while primitive traits are perceived as unattractive. Researchers utilized drawings and photographs to survey reactions from 495 subjects to a comparison of primitive vs. derived traits. The subjects were instructed to select the shape or proportion they considered more attractive. There was significant agreement among the subjects that derived anatomical traits were perceived as more attractive than primitive ones. According to the authors of this study, the Barbie doll is illustrative of how human beauty has evolved and indicates elements of human form that appear beautiful. The doll emphasizes our derived evolutionary traits and, possibly, that is why the doll is perceived as attractive.

Doctors and Their Patients

How far-reaching are the effects of beauty? A Texas Tech study documented the impact that beauty has on the relationship between a therapist and his or her patient. The researchers reviewed the existing literature that has consistently shown that patients judge their facially attractive therapists as more competent, trustworthy, genuine, and effective, when compared to less attractive therapists. The researchers from Texas looked at how a therapist's beauty affected their client's tendency to self-disclose in their therapy sessions. Clearly, a patient must feel free to disclose matters of a personal nature if psychological therapy is to be successful. The researchers found, "Most participants reported feeling more comfortable disclosing a benign (communication) problem than a potentially embarrassing (sexual) problem, and more comfortable disclosing problems to an attractive than to a less attractive female therapist." A question of major importance, not addressed in this study, involves whether or not there is a basis in fact for feeling generally more comfortable with an attractive therapist?

I have a unique perspective on this issue, because I simultaneously worked in the disparate worlds of the beauty business and the clinical setting of medicine and psychology. In the evening I consulted with female models and beauty pageant contestants, while during the day I fulfilled my fellowship requirements in medical psychology and plastic surgery. Virtually all of my clients in the evening were beautiful women. Some of them, as one might imagine, needed support or other therapeutic services, for which I made referrals to outside therapists. Without exception, my beautiful evening clients reported that their unattractive female therapists were jealous of them, which manifested as such behavior as condescension, rudeness, abruptness and general non-verbal expressions of competitive envy. Ultimately, I found an ex-beauty pageant winner who had gone on to become a family therapist, who agreed to see my referrals. My beautiful clients reported no such competitiveness issues with her. When making referrals to male therapists, I found that a number of them re-referred the client because of their own attractiveness to the client. Others, I regret to say, engaged in such seductive and inappropriate behavior, that the client became very uncomfortable and terminated the therapist/client relationship.

Part of my unique perspective on therapist/client-patient relationship dynamics comes from my analysis of my female supervisors in medicine and psychology. I noted, without looking for the pattern, that one of the more unattractive female psychologists consistently gave less attention to her attractive female patients. Not only did she give less attention to them, she went out of her way to be mean to them. The male doctors, on the other hand, treated the beautiful female patients with more attention and with more compassion. Just imagine what it is like to be a beautiful patient when your female doctors compete with you and use your vulnerabilities against you, while your male doctors shower you with attention. It is no wonder that many beautiful women trust men more than women, and that beautiful therapists may be easier to talk to, especially if you are an attractive woman.

Canadian researchers investigated the extent to which beauty affects a physician's perception of a patient's degree of pain. To quote from the study, "The results showed that physicians' ratings of pain were influenced both by attractiveness of patients and by nonverbal expressions of pain. Unattractive patients, and patients who were expressing pain, were perceived as experiencing more pain, distress, and negative affective experiences than attractive patients and patients who were not expressing pain. Unattractive patients also received higher solicitude on the doctor's part and lower ratings of health than attractive patients. Physician's assessments of pain appear to be influenced by the physical attractiveness of the patient."

Nation's Status

Beauty appears to act as a cue about the status of one's nation of origin, at least for the Japanese. A Japanese study found that research subjects tended to connect attractive people with nations of higher status. The moniker of "third world country" carries with it a stigma, as the term is used colloquially. Being presumed to have come from a nation of "lower status" can have many deleterious effects, but not for the beautiful. This phenomenon can be seen most clearly in international beauty pageants, where beauty has the ability to counterbalance the stigma associated with coming from a so-called nation of lower status. An analog of this phenomenon can be found to occur within the same culture. For example, women who come from so-called lower class backgrounds can move freely between social strata if they are beautiful, at least as far as men are concerned. No such social mobility appears to work with any degree of predictability for men who are "just" attractive.

Skin Color and Stereotype

In part one of a study conducted by researchers at Tufts University, college-age subjects from the greater Boston area were shown pictures of light- and dark-skinned black men and women. Subjects were then asked to match up a series of neutral statements with the photographs. In part two of the study, researchers asked subjects to list the traits they believed were commonly associated with light and dark-skinned black people. One of the more clever aspects of this study was a design that isolated skin tone from other physical cues, such as hair texture, lip fullness or nose width.

What the researchers found was that *both* black and white people ascribed differing descriptive adjectives to African-Americans according to the lightness or darkness of their skin. In addition to being judged as more attractive, lighter-skinned black people were judged to be more intelligent and more likely to possess wealth. Conversely, darker-skinned black people were judged to have less money, be tougher or more likely to be a criminal.

Dr. Keith Maddox, the lead author of the study, who happens to be of African-American decent, told a reporter for the Boston Globe, shortly after his work was published, that the subject area of his research has been thought of as divisive and explosive and something we shouldn't ever talk about in public. Dr. Maddox went on to say: "If you don't try to understand it, then things will never get better."

The purely sociological interpretation of these findings posits such results as a legacy of slavery, and all that has accompanied that miserable chapter in the history of the United States. The theory rests upon the notion that black people have been inculcated with so many negative descriptions over the last two hundred years in America that both black and white people subscribe to these negative descriptions. Perhaps a closer look at this study will tell us something about the effects of beauty.

By way of background, many of the students who served as the test subjects of this study were born in the 1980s. Many come from middle-class and privileged environments. The college-age young men and women who made up the test subjects of this research, if they are anything like the average white and black American, love Michael Jordan, Barry Bonds, Eddie Murphy, Chris Rock and are fans of numerous black rap artists. Furthermore, much to the chagrin of purists in the hip-hop culture, many of the white young men in the test subject pool, if they are anything like white young men across America, so admire hip-hop culture that they have adopted many of the mannerisms, speech, dress and attitudes associated with hip-hop culture. Add to these sociological data the fact that every person on Earth seems to ascribe positive adjectives to that which is beautiful. This phenomenon is so widespread that Dion, Berscheid and Walster entitled their landmark research in the early 1970's: "What is Beautiful is Good." People from all cultural backgrounds tend to ascribe more positive traits to good looks. In 1941, a researcher by the name of Monihan studied the perception of criminals by experienced workers in the criminal justice system. She concluded that even battle-hardened social workers find it hard to believe that beautiful women can be guilty of a crime, noting that people tend to think of criminals in terms of abnormality in appearance. If lighter-skinned people are perceived as more attractive and less threatening, as the Tuft's study data suggest, the question becomes, then, why are darker-skinned people less attractive, and is there a beauty connection?

A more sociobiological-beauty related interpretation of Dr. Maddox' research findings involves the visuo-spatial image processing associated with light-absorbing images versus light-reflecting images. Darker-skinned people lose some of their inherent three-dimensional beauty cues because of the loss of contrast-effect which is part and parcel to darker skin. And with regard to the "menacing" adjectives ascribed to darker-skinned people, e.g., "aggressive" and "tough," many of the facial cues which inform others of kinder intent and motive are lost to the observer who looks at a darker-skinned person. In the modeling business, "tanned" models are often described as "hard." People with mid-range skin tones are easier to see when compared to very dark-skinned people. Mid-range skin tones reflect more light, and the shading within their particular range of "lightness" affords a more vibrant contrast effect, when compared to a darker-skinned person.

If contrast effect and beauty cues account for some of the negative adjectives ascribed to darker-skinned people, wouldn't it follow that very light-skinned people would also suffer a similar prejudice? As a matter of fact, very light-skinned people are stereotyped with negative adjectives, not unlike their darker-skinned counterparts. And like their darker-skinned brothers and sisters, very light-skinned people, as for example albino populations, also lose much of their facial cue information related to beauty and those facial designs which inform others of a kinder intent, because of the loss of contrast which comes from a very light skin tone. Dr. Vail Reese, a San Francisco dermatologist, told "Wired News" about his research on the subject of albinism. Dr. Reese has chronicled the negative portrayal of albino men and women in movies. *Matrix: Reloaded*, aka *Matrix 2: Reloaded*, included villains known as "The Twins." Other more recent movies that have portrayed albinos as evil characters include *Star Wars: Episode II, Attack of the Clones*; *Tomorrow Never Dies*; *Blade 2 and Star Trek Nemesis*. The movie *The Time Machine*, included an entire race of albino creatures called "Morlocks." According to Dr. Reese, "audiences recognize it very quickly. They've learned that if you see a character with albinism in the movie, it's going to be an evil character. Its become part of the film language, for better or worse." (SEE PHOTO CREDITS OF ALBINISM IN THE MOVIES)

Assessment of overall health, an important social cue to others related to reproductive fitness and personal survival, is another factor related to man's attention to skin tone. A culture's reaction to skin color may have a sociobiological basis. On the Western Coast of Africa, Darwin wrote in his work *Descent of Man* that the natives admire a darker skin more than one of a lighter tint. Their horror of whiteness may be attributed as partly to their thinking it a sign of ill health. This assessment of health by equating it with various skin tones is absolutely accurate, both in Africa and the Western World. "Paleness" may mean low blood sugar, hypotension, disease or the blanching that frequently occurs just before a person vomits. "Green behind the gills" is a colloquialism that connotes poor health and unattractiveness as judged from skin tone and color.

191

A Few Examples of Albino Movie Villains

Photo: Andrew Cooper/Warner Brothers

"Uber" from *The Time Machine*

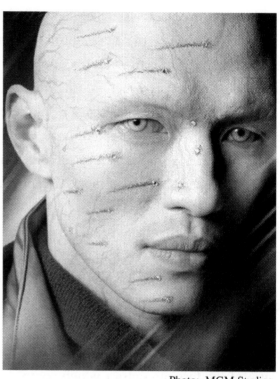

Photo: MGM Studios

"Zao" from *Tomorrow Never Dies*

Photo: Warner Brothers

"The Twins" from *Matrix 2: Reloaded*

Photo: Lucas Films

"Sly Moore" from *Star Wars: Episode II, Attack of the Clones*

Preferences for a particular skin tone and color may have little or nothing to do with deep-seated sociological processes. For example, fair-skinned white people who "tan" are never assumed to be motivated by some unconscious sociological motive related to race, e.g., white people who tan are so attracted to black culture that they want to share their skin tone. We do not ascribe a psychodynamic motive of identification to white people who tan, which would explain their desire to tan as an unconscious desire to identify with oppressed and negatively stereotyped darker-skinned people. No, white people who tan simply want to look good.

Researchers understand that by tanning a moderate amount, fair-skinned people increase the homogeneity of skin tone and even out blue and ashen shades which are unattractive to the eye. Similarly, black people who even out their skin tone or increase their luminosity and homogeneity by lightening their skin should not be understood as engaged in anything other than the quest for a marker of beauty that may have little or no relationship to cultural norms. It should be noted that, for example, when Eldoquin-Forte, a prescription skin lightener, is applied to both lighter and darker skin, its primary effect is to even out skin tone by "lifting" the dark spots that are the inevitable consequence of aging, exposure to sunlight and irregular pigmentation patterns in the human melanin complement. Thus, so-called skin-lightening cremes are more aptly thought of as skin-homogenization cremes. Good skin care, particularly skin care which increases homogeneity and clarity in skin tone, is associated with a dramatic increase in beauty. In fact, skin care, with particular reference to creating a healthy skin tone and color, offers the greatest "bang for the buck" when it comes to increasing attractiveness. When black people apply moisturizing lotion in order to avoid the ashen hues which occur when some darker skin becomes dry, they are not unconsciously or consciously trying to avoid becoming more like some of their anglo brethren, i.e., lighter, they simply want to look good.

Beauty and Achievement Related Traits

What appears to emerge time and time again is that being perceived as physically attractive is dramatically different for women as opposed to what it means for men. A study from East Carolina University looked at the effects of physical attractiveness and gender on perceptions of academic success, achievement-related traits, intelligence, initiative, and attributions of ability and effort in relation to academic success. The researchers found that "being perceived as physically attractive created positive impressions of achievement-related traits for men, but negative impressions for women." My own experience in the beauty pageant business informs me that the vast majority of the women who compete in pageants, especially at the regional and/or state level, are very intelligent and often have achieved a great deal of academic success. Regardless, it is very difficult for these women to be perceived as intelligent, especially by other less attractive women who have achieved academic and/or professional recognition. This study supports the proposition that attractive men are given the benefit of the doubt when it comes to their achievement-related abilities. On the other hand, if you happen to be a man whose only claim to fame is that you are attractive, then you are assumed to be lacking in the achievement-related traits examined in this study.

Consumer Behavior

In a study which evaluated the attitudes of graduate students at the University of Bombay, researchers examined the physical attractiveness stereotype in the context of consumer behavior, with physical attractiveness and clothing elegance as between-subject variables and type of consumer product as a within-subject variable. Female graduate students in India were shown photographs of a young female model and were asked to indicate the quality of four consumer products that the model was likely to choose. Product quality was rated higher for the attractive model than for the plain (non-attractive) model, but the difference was significant only for beauty products. Product quality was rated higher for the elegantly dressed model than for the model who was not elegantly dressed, irrespective of product type. At first glance, the findings make logical sense in that beautiful models would logically be associated with beauty-related products, such as cosmetics. But a closer look suggests that a well-dressed model increases the presumed quality of the product even if the product has nothing whatsoever to do with beauty, including clothing. What may be happening here is an attractiveness bias, wherein the primary credibility of a beautiful woman only involves issues and topics directly related to beauty.

Beauty and Aggression

A study conducted in New Rochelle, New York concluded, and I quote: "The influence of one's physical appearance is enormous, especially during social interactions with others." The researchers focused on the effect of beauty on aggressiveness during social encounters. According to the authors, undergraduate college participants, 40 men and 40 women, had water spilled on them as an aggression-provoking situation. All participants were rated for aggression by the two experimenters and by themselves. The main effect for attractiveness as observed by the experimenters was significant, with unattractive confederates having more aggression manifested toward them than toward their attractive peers. After reading this study I couldn't help but reflect upon all of those disenfranchised kids in high school who live in stark fear of dropping their lunch tray or tripping and spilling water on their more attractive counterparts, not to mention the scores and scores of physically unattractive kids described in our chapter, *Murderous Rage,* who have been the target for bullies across this nation and in every school.

The "Makeover"

In a study which supports the value of "makeovers," changing one's looks for the better can have a positive effect on interpersonal relations. A California State University study replicated what has been shown time and time again, "The research shows that improving a physical trait improves attitude, personality, and self-esteem. Likewise, improving physical attractiveness improves interpersonal interactions. These more positive interactions are internalized intrapersonally (within a person), with direct, corresponding impact on the person's self-esteem."

But one is left to ponder the fact that if interpersonal relations work better because you are pretty, as opposed to, for instance, that you are a more loving or giving person, then what is the true nature of the interpersonal relationship? Can physical attractiveness make up for poor interpersonal skills? The answer is no, but it is not quite that simple. In a study from the University of Nebraska, researchers found, and I quote: "Skilled behavior was viewed as more competent when performed by an attractive person compared to an unattractive person. Attractiveness had no influence on ratings of generally incompetent behavior. Thus, it appears that physical attractiveness does not compensate for poor interpersonal skills, but an attractive individual who also possesses good interpersonal skills may have an interpersonal advantage and be judged to have better skills even though those skills are similar to those possessed by their less attractive counterparts.

The Bargaining Process

In yet another study which looked at the often subtle effect of beauty, researchers studied how looks affect the bargaining process. These results are particularly important given the frequency with which people are required to bargain in their daily lives. Results revealed no significant differences in the offers or demands attractive and unattractive people made. However, attractive people were treated differently by others. Consistent with the notion of a "beauty premium," attractive people were offered more, but more was demanded of them. A gender difference was also apparent, with men more likely to be offered more, with less demanded of them.

What this study demonstrates is that all of the various benefits showered upon beautiful women come with a price. It appears that in many circumstances, the beautiful woman's life can be summed up as a quid pro quo. True, she may be offered more, as this study demonstrates, but more is then expected of her. True, a beautiful woman may have her choice of sexual partners, but not without the demand of having to provide her mate with an ever attractive and exciting sexual partner.

Children

As we have discussed throughout this book, children are bombarded with images related to beauty. In particular, we have noted the exposure that coming-of-age girls are subjected to in the

Western world and other places where the West's obsession with beauty has been exported. A California study looked at what may provide some hope for girls who suffer psychological damage from the depictions of atypically proportioned female models. Researchers from Southerern California College found that, "In contrast to earlier studies suggesting that self-concept is stable by late adolescence and therefore resistant to change, adolescent girls' ratings of self-attractiveness were significantly higher following exposure to printed advertisements employing attractive models who were overweight compared to those exposed to models who were not overweight." I will draw the reader's attention to the fact that this study made a concession to beauty when images of overweight but facially beautiful models were presented to overweight teen girls.

A French study demonstrated that adolescent French girls viewed their maturing bodies more critically than did their male counterparts. These researchers concluded that the experience of the body and the experience of relations with opposite sex peers are not built in the same way in girls and boys during adolescence. When heavier girls are depicted in the media, they are usually portrayed in unflattering ways. The stereotype of the heavier, bespectacled, less attractive, but intelligent sidekick of the beautiful girl, is a hackneyed character that one can only fully appreciate for the pain it causes if one looks at those depictions from the perspective of the heavier girl.

Researchers at the University of Houston looked at how the daughters of Mexican-Americans, ages 7-12 years, felt about their body type. Despite the fact that both obese and normal-sized mothers were satisfied with their daughter's body size, their daughters desired thinner figures than the one they currently had.

The effects of beauty affect kids in many subtle ways. A 1997 study from Purdue University looked into how adults speculated about preschoolersí levels of function based solely upon their looks. Unknown to the raters of the children's photographs, the children had been assessed for their level of social function by teachers using standardized tests. The researchers found, "dysfunctional children were easily distinguished from their competent peers. Specifically, dysfunctional children were rated as less attractive, more aggressive, more anxious, less socially competent, and more likely to have an emotional or behavioral problem than competent children."

Given that attractive children are generally treated better than their less attractive peers, one must consider the proverbial "chicken or egg" question. Dysfunctional kids are less attractive, but are they more dysfunctional, at least in part, because they are unattractive in the first place?

Children can be stereotyped for no other reason than wearing glasses. In a study from Bishop's University in Canada, kids who wore glasses were judged to be more intelligent, but duller, than their non-bespectacled counterparts.

In a study from Wesleyan University in Connecticut, parents of both sexes begin to give increasingly less positive evaluations on the dimension of physical attractiveness to their children as they age. At what age does this shift begin? In the Wesleyan study the researchers found parents down-rating their children's beauty as early as grade school.

What we usually find is that parents almost universally find their very young children attractive, and treat them that way. But it doesn't take long before parents begin to become less enamored with the looks of their children, when the "cuteness" wears off and is not replaced with natural beauty. Child actors, who are often hired because of their "cuteness," experience a similar phenomenon at the hands of the public as they age. Unfortunately, a lot of children receive adulation for something as transient as childhood attractiveness. None of these children ever presume that their "cuteness" will fade. But when it does, the withdrawal from all of the positive attention can be devastating.

Age

A Canadian study has explored the link between age and beauty. "Researchers studied 160 younger and older white Canadians and rated the attractiveness and personality traits of 1 of 4 target women. The results indicated an interaction between the participant's age and gender and the age and attractiveness of the target person. Both younger and older judges showed an attractiveness bias and down-rated the social desirability of younger, unattractive targets. Younger judges rated younger and older attractive targets as equal in social desirability. Older male judges rated older attractive targets as less socially desirable than younger attractive targets."

This study seems to confirm the inextricable relationship between youth and beauty. This relationship between youth and beauty has far-reaching consequences for how people interact with one another. We live in a society where being youthful is equated with vibrance and social desirability, the same characteristics ascribed to attractive women. Getting older, and therefore becoming less socially desirable, can be mitigated by maintaining one's beauty. Older males, however, possess views on youth and attractiveness that suggests both a prejudice against not only the unattractive woman, but older women who are attractive. Is it no wonder that we see older, unattractive men with power and/or wealth, with younger, attractive women.

Women between the ages of 61 and 92 were studied at the University of British Columbia. The researcher concluded that "The women in the study exhibit the internalization of ageist beauty norms even as they assert that health is more important to them than physical attractiveness."

Pretending Orgasm

In a study which looked at the issue of pretending orgasm during sexual intercourse and objective and subjective measures of facial beauty, the researchers found that of the 161 young adult women studied, more than half reported having pretended orgasm during sexual intercourse. Interestingly, the "pretenders" did not differ from the "non-pretenders" when it came to objective measures of facial attractiveness, but those women who were "pretenders" rated themselves, subjectively, as facially more attractive. They were also significantly older; reported having had first intercourse at a younger age; reported greater numbers of lifetime intercourse, fellatio, and cunnilingus partners; and scored higher on measures of sexual esteem and love of sex. The researchers concluded that only sexual esteem was uniquely related to having pretended orgasm. I suppose men would find it disconcerting, to say the least, to learn that if their sexual partners feel that they have pretty faces and possess high sexual esteem, that the response they get in bed may be more worthy of an Oscar nomination than a testament to their sexual prowess.

Gay and Lesbian Issues

Up until this point, research findings have focused upon heterosexual relationships. Are the effects of beauty different for gay and lesbian people? One interesting study looked at what gay men versus lesbian women find important in a prospective mate. Just like their heterosexual counterparts, gay men were more interested in pure sexuality and physical attractiveness. Lesbian women, on the other hand, more like their heterosexual counterparts, were more concerned with personality characteristics of prospective mates.

One interesting study from Sweden, utilizing research subjects from Berkeley, California, tested the "gay-pretty-boy" stereotype. To quote from the study: "Analysis showed that the 62 women rated 3 men as significantly more physically attractive when they believed the men were homosexual than when they believed the men were heterosexual. The 65 men did not rate photographs of 3 women as more physically attractive when they believed the women were lesbian compared to when they believed the women were heterosexual. The results illustrate an effect of the 'gay-pretty-boy stereotype,' namely, that women judged to be nonhomophobic perceived homosexual men as more physically attractive than comparable heterosexual men."

Gender Identity

In a study from Canada, six-year-old girls with gender identity disorder were evaluated by university students for five traits having to do with their physical attractiveness, i.e., attractive, beautiful, cute, pretty, and ugly. The evaluators had no idea which girls had been given the diagnosis of a gender identity disorder. The researchers found that the girls with gender identity disorder were significantly less attractive than those girls who did not suffer from a gender identity disorder.

An earlier study, from The Clarke Institute of Psychiatry in Canada, studied boys with a diagnosed gender identity disorder. The boys were evaluated by university students on five factors having to do with physical attractiveness, i.e., attractive, beautiful, cute, handsome, and pretty. Unlike the later study which found little girls with gender identity disorder to be less attractive than control children, the boys with the gender identity disorder were judged to be more attractive than control boys. This finding may be related to the "gay-pretty-boy stereotype."

Macho

Rich men and pretty women go together. It is also true that many wealthy men possess a "macho" attitude. In a study from Auburn University, researchers found that: "High macho subjects viewed females as less attractive than low macho subjects." Physical attractiveness of the male subjects was largely unrelated to their ratings of the females. Thus, men with a macho attitude are more critical of women when it comes to looks. Macho men who are unattractive, which is most often the case, categorize women according to their looks and are extremely critical, condescending and rude to unattractive women. As has been observed elsewhere, macho men are truly interested in beautiful women because "possessing" a beautiful woman makes the macho man more "macho." And to whom is the macho man more "macho?" Why, to other macho men, of course.

Chapter XVII: What Does It All Mean?

We began this book by noting the importance of beauty in all of our lives. There remains, however, a hidden effect that derives its power from beauty's remarkable ability to siphon time, emotional energy and intellectual attention from socially relevant issues. Young Americans spend more time thinking, worrying and engaging in beauty-related activities than they do caring for their family, their health, their emotional well-being, politics or just about anything else you can think of. One measure of the amount of time spent thinking about beauty is reflected in the amount of money America's youth spends on beauty related services and products. Teen Research Unlimited, a Chicago-based marketing company, reported that American teenagers spent $155 billion in the year 2000 on beauty-related products and services. That figure increased from $123 billion in 1997 and shows no sign of slowing down. To put that amount of money in perspective, according to the Pharmaceutical Manufacturer's Association, only $26 billion or so was spent by drug companies in the year 2000 for research and development into new drugs designed to treat illness. One can only imagine what benefits would occur if America's youth spent their money on something as mundane as intellectual development, rather than beauty-related products and services.

Teen girls, as a whole, spend more time trying to emulate Britney Spears and Christina Aguilara, or the most recent star du jour, than they do caring about their current and future health. In reality, the truth is much worse. Teens will harm their health and future survivability just so they can be pretty. Receiving a compliment about one's looks makes the average person feel better than complimenting them about their community service or their academic excellence.

One poignant example of how young women compromise their health and future survivability involves the relationship between tanning and skin cancer. In the year 2001, the American Cancer Society reported that the most frequent form of cancer for women between the ages of 25 and 29 is melanoma, the most deadly form of skin cancer. Over the last 25 hyper-image conscious years, the incidence of melanoma has increased 60 percent. Deborah Netburn researched the ever-increasing popularity of tanning among teen women when she wrote an investigative article in the summer of 2002 for the New York Times News Service. Netburn quoted Molly Nover, the beauty director of *Cosmo Girl*, a spin-off from *Cosmopolitan Magazine* that appeals to teen girls. Quoting Nover, Netburn wrote: "It started in 2000. The models in the Channel, Valentino and Guess ads that year were (sic) that savage tan. At the spring shows this year, they were putting shimmer creams on the models and mixing baby oil and bronzer." The editor of *Cosmo Girl*, Atoosa

Rubenstein, believes that singers Britney Spears and Christina Aguilera are 90 percent responsible for the teenage tanning trend. Netburn interviewed a teen girl from New York City who referred to herself as Miss Mary Sunshine. Netburn quoted her as saying, "When you think of getting ready for a party, you think, 'I'll get my hair done, get a manicure and go tanning.'" The reader is referred to our chapter entitled *Scientific Research* for a more complete discussion of some of the issues surrounding skin color.

The problem isn't just with our nation's youth. For example, here is a notice that appeared in a major American newspaper soliciting subjects for Alzheimer's research in the year 2001. The notice was captioned: "Wrinkles or Alzheimers?" The notice went on to read: "Amazing, but true, a recent magazine article reported that many older people valued a youthful appearance over how we think. They would rather look young and live without memory."

It is difficult to find fault with those who argue that women's emphasis upon beauty and making themselves physically attractive to men is the strongest of the invisible chains which hold women in bondage. This particular bondage has not only endured, but has gotten progressively worse, while other measures of exploitation, such as job discrimination, have lessened. Feminists who have drawn our attention to the beauty siphon phenomenon have been ridiculed for their lack of personal attractiveness, an ironic criticism considering the damned-if-you-are and damned-if-you-aren't double-binding prerequisite to commenting on the subject of beauty. The fact that Bella Abzug was less attractive than Gloria Steinem, for example, didn't water down either of their respective messages about the personal and social perils of spending one's time trying to be pretty rather than looking out for what is good for one's inner self and the community at large. Feminists have always known that if women put as much energy into protecting their rights as they did into worrying about their looks, the world would be a significantly friendlier place to women. Social observers are damned to even dare make note of the fact that more young women subscribe to Cosmopolitan than Scientific American. The fact that young women are likely to know more about the hair style of pop music idols than the politicians who control their lives, is such a given in today's world that no one seems to care.

Huge segments of the economy service those women who sell their beauty to men who can buy it. One is left to speculate how different the world would be if beauty were for sale only to those men who had dedicated their lives to the betterment of mankind. Consider, for a moment, how different the world would be if beautiful women refused to give the time of day to men whose most notable characteristic is the fact that they are wealthy. Or consider how different the world would be if men of wealth and power sought after women who were, above all else, beautiful on the inside. Consider how teen girls would spend their time if beauty didn't receive attention from boys and men. Could it be that by merely staring at a pretty girl, one is promulgating a process that destroys well-being and social responsibility? When women give voice to such ideas, they are labeled as radicals.

De-emphasizing beauty would destroy huge segments of the American economy. Such a de-emphasis, even if it were possible, is never going to happen. From a purely economic perspective, it appears clear that our collective obsession with acquiring and maintaining beauty is promoted, maintained and jealously protected by vested interests. People are made to feel insecure about their looks because creating that insecurity is good for business. Such insecurity is reinforced by a continual barrage of images of others who do not look normal, who are beautiful, happy, rich and living the good life. Once the market is created, a gazillion different products and services are sold to satiate the misery. The seller manipulates and preys upon one of mankind's oldest desires, to be desirable. "You will be desirable if you look good," is the underlying message in virtually all marketing strategies. Enough is never enough, however, because no matter how good you look, you are always being undermined and made to feel insecure by vested interests who need to always expand their market.

It is one thing to engineer planned obsolescence in an automobile in order to protect market share; it is quite another to engineer human insecurity in order to create the emotional void that ensures a continuing market for the newest, biggest, greatest, latest or best product that promises beauty, and thus desirability. Marketers always reply with the same mantra, "We only give the customer what they want." Those same marketers always, and very conveniently, refuse to accept responsibility for creating the very want that they cite as the raison d'être which justifies their marketing efforts. Billions upon billions of dollars are spent creating want in consumers. It is as though, once the heroin addict is created by injecting him with the drug, the act of selling heroin to that same addict is self-servingly described by the pusher as merely giving the addict what he or she wants.

There are a number of individuals who don't seem to be obsessed with physical beauty. All of these people have one thing in common: they are neither attractive nor unattractive. Virtually all of these people have charming and richly complex personalities. They are introspective and unconcerned about suntans, makeup, hair, nails, facial symmetry, weight, hair or any of the other markers which define beauty. Every one of them, to the person, has a spectacular sense of humor.

Individuals who do not seem to care about beauty consistently look inside themselves in order to find a sense of self-esteem and worth. Somehow, they have developed an immunity to a culture that equates self-worth with one's beauty. Not only do these individuals place little value on their own looks, they don't seem to respond to other's level of attractiveness. Men who fit into this category are remarkably unresponsive to beautiful women. Women in this group find it virtually impossible to even imagine what it would be like to be "desired" because of how she looks.

The process by which this type of person is allowed to develop is perhaps the most telling, with the key word being "allowed." The non descript-looking person may be able to "slip" through a very narrow safe harbor passage in our culture's obsessive emphasis upon beauty. By no means does merely being non descript-looking guarantee that you will escape our culture's intense psychological conditioning on the subject of beauty. Exposure to the media must be controlled, as well as one's inherent sensitivity to the messages imbedded within the various media. This person must have a very active internal life, and must be allowed to escape, for the most part, the horrendous pressures and influences that both unattractive and attractive individuals are subjected to.

Unattractive and attractive individuals are almost never spared the intense conditioning and psychological pressures that non descript-looking people can sometimes avoid. Unattractive and attractive individuals are subjected to differential treatment by others at an early age. Unattractive kids are picked on, harassed, made fun of, ostracized and acquainted with the feelings associated with being unpopular before they enter middle school. Attractive kids are subjected to the narcotic of attention and popular status, while at the same time blind-sided with jealousy, envy and competition from both unattractive and attractive kids. Teachers also subject unattractive and attractive kids to differential treatment. Attractive kids become heavily invested in their looks by the time they enter grade school. Attractive kids, right along with their unattractive counterparts, have their social roles defined for them.

Billy Crystal's character "Fernando" was fond of saying: "Better to look good than to feel good." Looking good while feeling bad, and vice versa, captures one of the greatest ironies associated with beauty. It is hard to feel good inside when you look good, because being attractive is at best a double-edged sword. When you are pretty, you are the person others love... to hate. On the other hand, not looking good is a handicap that makes it hard to feel good inside, especially if you are a woman.

Knowing about the importance of beauty begs for a more socially responsible way of living with our culture's love of beauty. Ignoring the importance of beauty is not the answer, but neither is our culture's narcissistic emphasis upon beauty. It may be the wiser choice to begin to reassert the old adage: "pretty is as pretty does."

People can change. And while beauty will always cast its magic spell, we can compensate for our feelings and we can become more aware. As we have already discussed in our chapter entitled *The Cult of the Beautiful Egg*, sexuality and beauty are inextricably linked. When it comes to compensating for the negative influence of beauty, men and women have different burdens.

Men of means must stop paying for women who are beautiful, either just because or mostly because they are pretty. The practice of "paying for beauty," whether it is a mail-order bride, the women who scout professional athletes, beauty pageant winners, or the homecoming queen in high school, must be tempered. Men must emphasize personality and character BEFORE giving expression to their love of beauty. The reader will notice that I state BEFORE giving expression to their infatuation with beauty. I recognize that the love of beauty is almost overwhelming. Just because someone is beautiful does NOT mean that she is entitled to share in another person's material wealth. To say it another way, poor character and a poor personality should become a "deal breaker" when dealing with a beautiful woman.

Women must stop selling their beauty to the highest bidder. Parents must help little girls understand the profound difference between receiving attention because of "it" and receiving attention for uniquely personal reasons. Beautiful mothers, in particular, must recognize that men look at "it" and not the person. Nothing is special about getting attention from men because you possess beauty. Nothing is special about getting a man to buy you things because you are beautiful. And pretty girls never get something for nothing. And of course, what is required of beautiful girls and women is for them to break through their defenses which always insist, with monotonous consistency, that "beauty is not the reason he is with me."

The world is full of unattractive people who are getting even for their lack of popularity and their jealousy of attractive people, whether it is the child murderer who kills, the academician who relishes the exercise of capricious power over her attractive intern, or the politician or political zealot who must bring down an attractive sitting president. The "get even" motive is everywhere we look. Each and every social institution and cultural ritual that idealizes that which is attractive, at the expense of those left out, sows the seeds of future misery. Sadly, real life is all too much like high school.

Jealousy of attractive people should be recognized as a very common problem, one with dire consequences. Unattractive people who make a career of regulating the sexual behavior of others should closely examine their motives. Attractive people who are also intelligent should not be punished, shackled or allowed to become the target of passive-aggressive supervisors, bosses, leaders or peers. People who play upon our universal love of that which is beautiful should not be able to manipulate consumers without their full awareness. Consumers should be able to point out each and every manipulative tactic which incorporates the beauty factor. And finally, we all should examine our love of the aphid dragon over the praying mantis.

As I wrote in the very beginning, beauty is one of those subjects that always seems to get attention. Over the years, beauty has garnered the attention of poets, playwrights, politicians, pundits and a host of other people who gave expression to their thoughts and feelings about beauty. I will leave you with the following quotations, all on the subject of beauty:

If you're considered a beauty, it's hard to be accepted doing anything but standing around.
....Cybil Shepard

What ever beauty may be, it has for its basis order, and for its essence unity.
....Father Andre Tara Grady

Beauty is only skin deep, but it's a valuable asset if you're poor or haven't any sense
....Kin Hubbard

She was a beauty in her youth a fact which she alone remembers
....Benjamin Constant

The beauty that addresses itself to the eyes is only the spell of the moment, the eye of the body is not always that of the soul
....George Sand

Compliments invite the person who is complimented to embrace a new perception of him or herself. And just as layers and layers of nacre form a pearl over an irritating grain of sand, so compliments collect around us, developing us in all our beauty.
....Daphne Rose Kingma

Beauty of style and harmony and grace and good rhythm depend on simplicity
....Plato

A thing of beauty is a joy forever: Its loveliness increases; it will never pass into nothingness.
....John Keats

Beauty is all very well at first sight; but who ever looks at it when it has been in the house three days?
....George Bernard Shaw

I'm tired of all this nonsense about beauty being only skin-deep. That's deep enough. What do you want....an adorable pancreas?
....Jean Kerr

The most common error made in matters of appearance is the belief that one should disdain the superficial and let the true beauty of one's soul shine through. If there are places on your body where this is a possibility, you are not attractive....you are leaking.
....Fran Lebowitz

The real sin against life is to abuse and destroy beauty, even one's own....even more, one's own, for that has been put in our care and we are responsible for its well-being
....Katherine Anne Porter

To me, fair friend, you never can be old for as you were when first your eye I eyed, Such seems your beauty still.
....William Shakespeare

Time may be a great healer, but it's a lousy beautician
....Unknown

Beauty is an ecstasy; it is as simple as hunger. There is really nothing to be said about it. It is like the perfume of a rose: you can smell it and that is all.
....Somerset Maugham

Beauty seen is never lost, God's colors all are fast.
....John Greenleaf Whittier

By plucking her petals, you do not gather the beauty of the flower.
....Rabindrath Tagore

Anyone who keeps the ability to see beauty, never grows old.
....Franz Kafka

Beauty in things exists in the mind which contemplates them.
....David Hume

Those who look for beauty, find it.
....Unknown

The ugly may become beautiful, the pretty never.
....Unknown

As a white candle in a holy place, So is the beauty of an aged face.
....Joseph Campbell

The pursuit of truth and beauty is a sphere of activity in which we are permitted to remain children all our lives.
....Albert Einstein

The ever-present phenomenon ceases to exist for our senses. It was a city dweller, or a prisoner, or a blind man suddenly given his sight, who first noted natural beauty.
....Remy de Gourmont

Anything in any way beautiful derives its beauty from itself and asks nothing beyond itself. Praise is no part of it, for nothing is made worse or better by praise.
....Marcus Aurelius

We ascribe beauty to that which is simple; which has no superfluous parts; which exactly answers its end; which stands related to all things; which is the mean of many extremes.
....Ralph Waldo Emerson

There is certainly no absolute standard of beauty. That precisely is what makes its pursuit so interesting.
....John Kenn

I look forward to an America which will not be afraid of grace and beauty.
....John Fitzgerald Kennedy

The beautiful remains so in ugly surroundings.
....Chazal

Let us worry about beauty first, and truth will take care of itself.
....A. Zee

Beauty is a fruit which we look at without trying to seize it.
....Simone Weil

Beauty and sadness always go together. Nature thought beauty too rich
to go forth upon the earth without a meet alloy.
....George MacDonald

Beauty comes in all sizes, not just size 5.
....Roseanne

Always remember that true beauty comes from within, not from within bottles, jars, compacts,
and tubes.
....Peter's Almanac

It's beauty that captures your attention; personality which captures your heart.
Anonymous

The absence of flaw in beauty is itself a flaw.
....Havelock Ellis

In nature, nothing is perfect and everything is perfect. Trees can be contorted, bent in weird
ways, and they're still beautiful.
....Alice Walker

If eyes were made for seeing, then Beauty is it's own excuse for being.
....Ralph Waldo Emerson

The truth isn't always beauty, but the hunger for it is.
....Nadine Gordimer

A thing of beauty is a joy forever; its loveliness increases; it will never pass into nothingness.
....John Keats

There is certainly no absolute standard of beauty. That precisely is what makes its pursuit so
interesting.
....John Kenneth Galbraith

Man makes holy what he believes, as he makes beautiful what he loves.
....Ernest Renan

The real sin against life is to abuse and destroy beauty, even one's own beauty even more, for that has been put in our care and we are responsible for its well-being.
....Katherine Anne Porter

Beauty deprived of its proper foils and adjuncts ceases to be enjoyed as beauty, just as light deprived of all shadows ceases to be enjoyed as light.
....John Ruskin

I learned the truth at seventeen that love was meant for beauty queens and high school girls with clear-skinned smiles who married young and then retired. The valentines I never knew, the Friday night charades of youth were spent on one more beautiful. At seventeen I learned the truth.

And those of us with ravaged faces, lacking in the social graces, desperately remained at home, inventing lovers on the phone, who called to say, "Come dance with me," and murmured vague obscenities. It isn't all it seems at seventeen.

A brown-eyed girl in hand-me-downs whose name I never could pronounce, said, "Pity, please, the ones who serve; they only get what they deserve. The rich relationed hometown queen marries into what she needs, a guarantee of company and haven for the elderly."

Remember those who win the game lose the love they sought to gain. In debentures of quality and dubious integrity. Their small-town eyes will gape at you in dull surprise when payment due, exceeds accounts received at seventeen.

To those of us who know the pain of valentines that never came, and those whose names were never called when choosing sides for basketball. It was long ago and far away; the world was much younger than today, and dreams were all they gave away for free to ugly duckling girls like me.

We all play the game and when we dare to cheat ourselves at solitaire. Inventing lovers on the phone, repenting other lives unknown, that call and say, "Come dance with me," and murmur vague obscenities, at ugly duckling girls like me at seventeen.
....Janice Ian (At Seventeen)

THE END

Bibliography

Abed, R.T. The sexual competition hypothesis for eating disorders. Department of Psychiatry, Rotherham District General Hospital, U.K.. British Journal of Medical Psychology 1998 December; 71 (Pt 4):525-547.

Alcock D., Solano J., Kayson W.A. How individuals' responses and attractiveness influence aggression. Psychological Reports 1998 June; 82 (3, Pt 2):1435-1438.

Becker, Anne. Eating behaviours and attitudes following prolonged television exposure among ethnic Fijian adolescent girls. British Journal of Psychiatry 2002; 180:509-514.

Berry, Diane S, Miller, Katherine M. When Boy Meets Girl: Attractiveness and the Five-Factor Model in Opposite-Sex Interactions. Journal of Research in Personality 2001 March; 35 (1): 62-67.

Burt, D.M., Perrett, D.I. Perceptual asymmetries in judgments of facial attractiveness, age, gender, speech and expression. Neuropsychologia 1997 May; 35 (5): 685-693.

Carroll, S.T., Riffenburgh, R.H., Roberts, T.A., Myhre, E.B. Tattoos and body piercings as indicators of adolescent risk-taking behaviors. Pediatrics 2002 June; 109 (6): 1021-1027.

Chia, R.C., Allred, L.J., Grossnickle, W.F., Lee, G.W. Effects of attractiveness and gender on the perception of achievement-related variables. Journal of Social Psychology 1998 August; 138 (4): 471-477.

Crouch, A., Degelman, D. Influence of female body images in printed advertising on self-ratings of physical attractiveness by adolescent girls. Perceptual Motor Skills 1998 October; 87 (2): 585-586.

Darwin, C. Descent of Man, 1871. Part III, Chapter 19. (on-line copy available at www.literature.org).

DeJong, W. Rape and physical attractiveness: judgments concerning likelihood of victimization. Psychological Reports 1999 August; 85 (1): 32-34.

Dion, K., Berscheid, K. and Walster, E. "What Is Beautiful Is Good," Journal of Personality and Social Psychology 1972; 24 (3): 285-290.

Fridell, S.R., Zucker, K.J., Bradley, S.J., Maing, D.M. Physical attractiveness of girls with gender identity disorder. Archives of Sexual Behavior 1996 February; 25 (1): 17-31.

Hadjistavropoulos, H.D., Ross, M.A., Von Baeyer, C.L. Are physicians' ratings of pain affected by patients' physical attractiveness? Social Science Medicine 1990; 31 (1): 69-72.

Hale, Sarah. Undergarment Trend Gets New Cheeky Exposure. Los Angeles Times, April 5, 2001.

Hall, S.K., Cousins, J.H., Power, T.G. Self-concept and perceptions of attractiveness and body size among Mexican-American mothers and daughters. International Journal of Obesity 1991 September; 15 (9): 567-575.

Harris, S.M., Busby, D.M. Therapist physical attractiveness: an unexplored influence on client disclosure. Journal of Marital Family Therapy 1998 April; 24 (2): 251-257.

Hatala, M.N., Prehodka, J. Content analysis of gay male and lesbian personal advertisements. Psychological Reports 1996 April; 78 (2): 371-374.

Heid, Jim. iBook loses its bulk, packs on the pixels. Los Angeles Times: Mac Focus, June 7, 2001.

Hope, D.A., Mindell, J.A. Global social skill ratings: measures of social behavior or physical attractiveness? Behaviour Research and Therapy 1994 May; 32 (4): 463-469.

Hurd, L.C. Older women's body image and embodied experience: an exploration. Journal of Women Aging 2000; 12 (3/4): 77-97.

Innala, S.M., Ernulf, K.E. When gay is pretty: physical attractiveness and low homophobia. Psychological Reports 1994 June; 74 (3, Pt. 1): 827-831.

Keisling, B.L., Gynther, M.D. Male perceptions of female attractiveness: the effects of targets' personal attributes and subjects' degree of masculinity. Journal of Clinical Psychology 1993 March; 49 (2): 190-195.

Kowner, R. Effect of group status on physical attractiveness preferences-from the Japanese case to a general cognitive perspective. Genetic, Social and General Psychology Monographs 1996 May;122 (2): 215-248.

Maddox, K.B., Gray, S. Cognitive representations of African Americans: re-exploring the role of skin tone. Personality and Social Psychological Bulletin 2002 February; 28 (2): 250-259.

Magro, A.M. Why Barbie is perceived as beautiful. Perceptual and Motor Skills 1997 August; 85 (1): 363-374.

McKelvie, S.J. Perception of faces with and without spectacles. Perceptual and Motor Skills 1997 April; 84 (2): 497-498.

Mealey, L., Bridgstock, R., Townsend, G.C. Symmetry and perceived facial attractiveness: a monozygotic co-twin comparison. Journal of Personality and Social Psychology 1999 January; 76 (1): 151-158.

Monihan, F. Women in Crime. New York: Ives Washburn, 1941.

Mojdehi, G.M., Gurtner, J. "Childhood lead poisoning through kohl." American Journal of Public Health 1996 April, 86 (4): 587-588.

Parekh, H., Kanekar, S. The physical attractiveness stereotype in a consumer-related situation. Journal of Social Psychology 1994 June; 134 (3): 297-300.

Patzer, G.L. Improving self-esteem by improving physical attractiveness? Journal of Esthetic Dentistry 1997; 9 (1): 44-46.

Perlini, A.H., Bertolissi, S., Lind, D.L. The effects of women's age and physical appearance on evaluations of attractiveness and social desirability. Journal of Social Psychology 1999 June; 139 (3): 343-354.

Rodriguez-Tome H., Bariaud, F., Zardi, M.F., Delmas, C., Jeanvoine, B., Szylagyi, P. The effects of pubertal changes on body image and relations with peers of the opposite sex in adolescence. Journal of Adolescence 1993 December; 16 (4): 421-438.

Salusso-Deonier, C.J., Markee, N.L., Pedersen, E.L. Gender differences in the evaluation of physical attractiveness ideals for male and female body builds. Perceptual and Motor Skills 1993 June; 76 (3 Pt. 2): 1155-1167.

Scheib, J.E., Gangestad, S.W., Thornhill, R. Facial attractiveness, symmetry and cues of good genes. Proceedings of the Royal Society of London, Biological Sciences 1999 September 22; 266 (1431): 1913-1917.

Serketich, W.J., Dumas, J.E. Adults' perceptions of the behavior of competent and dysfunctional children based on the children's physical appearance. Behavioral Modification 1997 October; 21 (4): 457-469.

Singh, D. Adaptive significance of female physical attractiveness: role of waist-to-hip ratio. Journal of Personality and Social Psychology 1993 August; 65 (2): 293-307.

Solnick, S.J., Schweitzer, M.E. The Influence of Physical Attractiveness and Gender on Ultimatum Game Decisions. Organizational Behavior Human Decision Process 1999 September; 79 (3): 199-215.

Striegel-Moore, R.H., Kearney-Cooke, A. Exploring parents' attitudes and behaviors about their children's physical appearance. International Journal of Eating Disorders 1994 May; 15 (4): 377-385.

Summers, Anthony. Goddess: The Secret Lives of Marilyn Monroe. New York: Macmillan., 1985.

Tovee, M.J., Maisey, D.S., Emery, J.L., Cornelissen, P.L. Visual cues to female physical attractiveness? Proceedings of the Royal Society of London, Biological Sciences 1999 January 22; 266 (1415): 211-218.

Townsend, J.M., Wasserman, T. The perception of sexual attractiveness: sex differences in variability. Archives of Sexual Behavior 1997 June; 26 (3): 243-268.

Weiss, Kenneth, R. "Eggs Buy a College Education." Los Angeles Times, May 27, 2001.

Wiederman, M.W. Pretending orgasm during sexual intercourse: correlates in a sample of young adult women. Journal of Sex and Marital Therapy 1997 Summer; 23 (2): 131-139.

Zucker, K.J., Wild, J., Bradley, S.J., Lowry, C.B. Physical attractiveness of boys with gender identity disorder. Archives of Sexual Behavior 1993 February; 22 (1): 23-36.

Index

CPSIA information can be obtained
at www.ICGtesting.com
Printed in the USA
BVHW091205191221
624339BV00009B/564

9 781589 393783